THE
WARLIZARD
CHRONICLES
Adventures with Vodka, Woman & War

"You're one of the most interesting people I've ever come across in the internet before... That what fascinates me the most is your writing."

"You tell all women that story? You should wash your mouth!"

"I think I could listen to your stories for hours."

"So you owe your marriage to the people who brought down the world trade center?"

"I have nothing else I can add or ask, except MORE STORIES."

"Holy shit. I wish I was you."

"Man, you're an inspiration, seriously. Fuck Tucker Max, you're the real shit. I'm sure to remember your stories whenever there's a choice to do some crazy shit. I used to say I'd do it for the lulz, now I'm gonna do it like WarLizard."

"Dear Mrs. Warlizard, while that was without doubt especially offensive and graphic, it was truthful. There aren't many men who would be that honest within earshot (so to speak) of their wives."

"Oh man, I was with you on all your stories until this one. You slept with another man's wife and then lied to him about it, and can say with a straight face it was the right thing?"

"Goddammit, I spewed out laughter too loud at work, now I have to leave because everyone knows I'm not doing shit. Fuck this is hilarious, and disconcerting, at the same time."

"He is the most interesting man in the world."

"Ok guys, I'm calling troll. Everyone knows lizards can't type."

"How old are you? I feel like a failure reading these stories, they're awesome."

"Your life experience makes me feel good. You good sir are somewhat of a new idol of mine. Nothing much you can do about that. Have a good day sir."

"You know if you were to hire someone with awesome writing talent, no matter how much talent they would have they would not be able to top this."

"Warlizard doesn't always drink beer, but when he does, he prefers Dos Equis."

"I just can't wrap my mind around the fact that not only a story like this exists but that a Reddit regular would be living it. And it kinda has this enthusiastic 'and then it happened...' moments in it that kinda style like you'd write fiction on the go."

"This guy is either the most creative man in the world or the most interesting man in the world. Either way..."

"You hate everyone and you can write really well. If you didn't have a family, you could become Spider Jerusalem!"

THE WARLIZARD CHRONICLES

Adventures with Vodka, Woman & War

By Warlizard

Warlizard Ink, LLC
www.Warlizard.com

© 2011, Warlizard®
All rights reserved. No part of this book may be reproduced in any form or by any electronic or mechanical means, including information storage and retrieval systems, without permission in writing from the publisher, except by a reviewer who may quote brief passages in a review.

First published by Warlizard 2011

For inquiries about volume orders, please contact:
Warlizard Ink, LLC
info@warlizard.com

Printed in the United States Of America
ISBN-13: 978-0615461878 (paperback)
ISBN-10: 0615461875

Cover Photo By Scottsdale Images
www.ScottsdaleImages.com

Disclaimer:
All names (unless specifically mentioned) have been modified or changed completely. Certain dates, locations, people and characteristics of these stories may have been changed to protect Warlizard from criminal prosecution or civil liability. And of course, any illegal activities mentioned in this book are here for entertainment purposes only and could never have happened. Also, do not try this at home. Void where prohibited. Use only in well-ventilated area. Well, you get the idea.

Contents

Introduction	XI
Some Stories	1
1. Betty	3
2. Cheating and Winning A Kissing Contest	23
3. How LSD got me ready for War	34
4. War	39
5. The French Girl	53
6. The Married Girl	55
7. The Arrest	59
8. My CoWorkers Prank Me Good	66
9. Leaving DLI	68
10. The German Redlight District	70
11. Always Buy the Ticket!	75
12. The "Spread"sheet	80
13. I Lose	86
14. Learn to Shoot Pool.	92

BAD ADVICE   99

15. Go Out and LIVE   101
16. "That's Not Fair"   103
17. I Really Like This Girl But She's Out of My League   105
18. Keep Your Mouth Shut, or the Virtue of Discretion   106
19. Quick Tech Support Tip   108
20. Get Some Checkboxes   109
21. SMILE   111
22. Learn to Grill a Steak   112
23. If You REALLY want a Job…   114
24. Talk to Everyone   116
25. There Are Good Times to Lie   117
26. I'm Bored, What Can I Do To Pass the Time?   118
27. You Don't Get To Be Friends With Him!   120
28. Are People Who Like Guns Crazy?   122
29. Career Path   124
30. What is Happiness?   127
31. Dirty Talk   130

BACK TO THE STORIES   133

32. Back in the Saddle   135
33. Celebrity Sighting   139
34. Parker   141
35. Breaking Up Using Porn   145
36. The Irish Girl   153

37.	The Twisted Ostrich	155
38.	The Greatest Lie I Ever Told	161
39.	I Run From The Cops	163
40.	Plug in the Strobe Light	168
41.	The Old Annoying Guy	171
42.	Getting Even	173
43.	The Feminist	181
44.	My Last Fight	185
45.	The Pathological Liar	187
46.	How I Got My First Book Published	194
47.	Muttface	198
48.	My First Job	207
49.	Never Settle.	210

AFTERWARD	221

INTRODUCTION

People always tell me I've had a crazy life and they're right. I've lived all over the world, met some wonderful people, and I've had the time of my life.

But it didn't happen by accident.

Every single time an opportunity was presented to me, I took it. Every time. I took every job offer, dated every girl, went on every trip, made every friend, did the flaming shot someone bought, took the train instead of the plane, and it led me to places I never could have imagined.

Was it fun to live through such utter insanity? Sure! I mean, I nearly married a girl whose "love" of dogs was illegal in 30 states, but I also won the heart of the girl of my dreams. My life has been the greatest adventure I could have imagined!

Now, did I do it right? Is this the best way to live? The jury is still out, but I'm here now, loving my life and happy as a clam with everything I hoped for and more. I jumped through every door with my eyes wide open, hoping for something fun on the other side. You don't do that, you may as well be dead.

-- Warlizard --

SOME STORIES

1. BETTY

My new fiancée Betty and I were sitting on the couch, watching the Westminster Kennel Club dog show when she looked over at me and casually said, "My first orgasm came from a dog."

As I sat there stunned, trying to control my reactions and collect myself, I had two immediate thoughts:

1. Now I know why my dog likes her better.
2. I wish this were the worst thing she'd ever told me.

Our relationship started as a blind date. My buddy was dating Betty's twin sister and one day he asked if I wanted to go out and party with the three of them. It was obviously a setup and since my history with blind dates was less than stellar, I hesitated. The last one I'd been on ended up with me pushing a very cute and giggling girl in a shopping cart, hitting a speed-bump, and watching her catapult out to faceplant on the asphalt. Tears and blood flowed freely and I didn't get a second date.

But hey, you only live once so I told him I was up for it. We arranged to meet at the Village Idiot, a bar in downtown Columbia, SC and from the moment I saw Betty, I was smitten.

She was just so much fun! If you've ever met someone who was the center of attention and the life of the party the moment they arrive, you'll know what I mean. Betty was an unstoppable force of nature and I really had no idea what I was in for.

We'd spent the last few hours drinking shots of something blue and laughing our asses off. Things were going really well but I didn't know how well until Betty looked up at me with a mischievous grin and said, "You wanna go back to your place and fuck?"

Even as wrecked as I was, it took me less than a second to answer.

"Hell yeah! Let's go!"

As I followed her down the stairs and watched her tight gymnast's ass, I thought I'd hit the lotto. Betty was bouncy and crazy, had a wide smile and was always happy. She was a fitness freak and her body showed it. Who wouldn't want a girl like that? I knew I did.

Over the next few weeks we were inseparable, and by that I mean we spent the next few weeks in bed. I liked the fact that she was completely open about sex and was unashamed to admit it. Most of the other girls at my school played it by the book and waited the requisite 3 dates before having sex. The dates were always formal and the girls habitually ordered the most expensive thing on the menu. Three dates later when they finally dropped panties, they expected me to fawn over them like they were letting me into Narnia. Just once I wanted to scream, "EVERY WOMAN IN THE WORLD HAS ONE! THERE'S NOTHING SPECIAL ABOUT YOURS."

I did not. But I wanted to. So you'll understand why Betty was so refreshing. She enthusiastically and loudly enjoyed sex and had no problem telling me when she was horny. It was a nice change. Sex was pretty vanilla initially, until I found a giant box of dildos and porn under her bed. My idiot mutt had crawled under there and was scratching at the box so of course I had to look inside.

What struck me most was not that she had *a* vibrator, but that she had so *many* of them. Large, small, ribbed, veined, black, pink, she had them all, in shapes not found in nature. I could only guess at how much she spent in batteries every month. But even that wasn't as crazy as her porn stash. Instead of magazines, she had paperbacks and by the wear and tear on them, they'd been read more than once.

I'll be honest – the topics were … a bit extreme. Most were borderline S&M, but quite a few of them had to do with naughty schoolgirls and their teachers, naughty daughters and their dads, naughty nieces and their uncles, and judging by the explicit covers, all the young ladies had been disobedient and required spankings.

Hey, you don't need to hit me over the head with a brick. I saw the recurring theme, so the next time we fooled around, I gave her a light smack on the ass. You'd think I hit the turbo button. She went nuts. It turned out she loved everything to do with her ass. Everything. The purpose of the smaller dildos became abundantly clear shortly thereafter.

At first this was fun, in the "OMG I am dating a freak!" but it got old pretty quick. Turned out, I didn't want to shove something up her ass every time we fooled around. If I didn't get a finger or a dildo or SOMETHING in there, she took forever to come. As a result, instead of it being something kinda dirty and fun, anything ass-related became a chore. There were no "special occasion" things that she'd do — everything was "on the menu", all the time.

As our relationship developed I found out more and more about her. She worked at a vet's office helping inseminate dogs. Her specific role was to extract the semen from the male. Yep, my girlfriend's job was to jack off dogs. Ok, bit of a setback, but nothing a well-laid boyfriend can't handle, right? We were partying like crazy and having a blast, so I could overlook an odd quirk here and there.

After a few months of being together, she really started to open up. She told me that her last boyfriend blindfolded her, tied her face down on the bed, and let his friends come in and do anything they wanted to her. She thought this was awesome and a huge turn-on.

In any relationship, you make sacrifices and allowances. It takes courage to just come out and tell your partner what turns you on, especially if it's a bit offbeat, so I didn't recoil in disgust or tell her she was crazy when she told me this. I just laughed and told her I was out of rope.

To be honest, it was disconcerting. I didn't like thinking of my girlfriend as some anonymous girl face-down getting hammered by a string of high-fiving gym-rats, but I figured that maybe it was all in the past. She was with me now and I wasn't into sharing.

Of course, I was dying to know what was going on in her head. Most of her fantasies involved submission and degradation and I wondered why. There had to be some psychological trigger in her little pea-brain and I started actively searching for it.

Although she still had her own apartment, Betty spent 90% of her time in my house and even had her own key. I came home one day and found her employing two dildos and a vibrator, riveted by the porn on the TV. Her claim that my house was "more private" and that's why she was always there made more sense.

You might think I would have flipped out walking in on that but I didn't and maybe it was because of Betty's reaction. She wasn't ashamed, didn't stop, and after she'd finished, gave me a big grin and said, "Wow, I came really hard. Now it's your turn." How can you get mad at that?

My whole relationship with Betty was so unique. Not only had I never dated anyone like her, I'd never MET anyone like her. I mean seriously, how many girls do you know who love porn and are confident enough to admit it?

Most of my former girlfriends liked bubble baths, candles and romance novels. Not Betty. She wanted gang-bangs, beatings, multi-penetration and humiliation. We started talking about her porn collection and decided that since it was so out of date, we should update it. We went online and I told her to get anything that looked interesting. It turned out our definitions of "interesting" were light years apart.

When the giant box of CDs, books, and videos arrived, I realized just how much our tastes differed. My idea of scandalous was a naughty schoolgirl. Hers involved physical pain and actual damage. One favorite story of hers had some guy kidnapping a girl and torturing her in his dungeon. He ends up squirting boiling oil into this girl's vagina and she dies from the pain. Betty loved it.

I still hadn't found the trigger, the reason why this particular type of fantasy was such a turn-on to her and it was driving me crazy. I didn't have anyone I could ask or talk to about it. Wikipedia was still more than a decade away. I would have to wait.

We'd been dating a few more months and I'd become somewhat used to her kinks. Hey, she was still fun, still crazy in bed and if she liked to think about getting raped and murdered when we had sex, who was I to judge? I guess the fact I accepted this about her made her feel more comfortable with me and she "mentioned" that when she was 14 she had become pregnant and had an abortion.

This was obviously something that was pretty secret and she watched me closely to see my reaction. You have to understand – we were in the Deep South, where "good girls" would never do such a thing. I told her that it must have been a very difficult decision and I could only imagine what it must have been like. I guess my answer was acceptable.

Betty and I had clearly reached a new stage in our relationship. I'd passed her test, so after telling me this, she said she wanted me to meet her family. I already knew her twin sister – she, her boyfriend, Betty, and I hung out constantly. But meeting her Mom and Dad was a big deal. I wasn't too sure this was a good idea, mostly because Betty clearly had her issues, but there really wasn't any way to avoid it and I figured I may as well. Might be fun, right?

I like people from the South but they have odd notions of what's acceptable and what isn't. I didn't know her mother had 2 other kids from a previous marriage but this was a bit of a scandal. Even worse, Betty had an older sister who lived in the projects and had a half-black kid. This may seem like nothing to you and to me, but I realized why it was a big deal when I met her parents.

Her Dad was an Old-School southern gentleman from Mississippi and his racism, while understated was clear. So his step-daughter having a half-black child was huge. The fact that she lived in the projects was even a bigger deal, since the parents were pretty well-off. Well, at least I thought they were and it wasn't until months later that I learned the truth.

Her brother, the other child from the first marriage, was borderline retarded. The first time I met him he was about 3 hours into a 2-tab acid trip. I never saw him when he wasn't under the influence of something and his life was one long, unbroken string of failures. Nothing he did succeeded. Still hasn't.

Racism aside, the dad was awesome. He laughed easily, made sure I always had a drink in my hand, had a string of hilarious stories and grilled one of the best steaks I'd ever eaten. Betty adored him. In college, he lived the life everyone wanted. He drove around town in a flashy red convertible, came from a wealthy family and was the object of every ambitious girl's affection.

As the proverbial "good catch", he had the his choice of any girl he wanted. The fact that he married a woman with 2 kids at a time when divorced women were often viewed with suspicion and contempt set off some alarm bells.

My buddy later speculated that the mother must have done something so wild and freaky that the dad just *had* to marry her to keep it coming. It made sense – like mother like daughter, right?

Actually, come to think of it, they shared quite a few similarities. Betty was a miniature version of her mom, but an inoffensive one. She liked to drink, but the mom was a sloppy, annoying, stumbling drunk, and I couldn't stand her. I played the part however and everyone thought I was wonderful. Turns out if you just smile, laugh, and let people talk, they like you.

A few months later, Betty told me that her parents were almost bankrupt. This was a shock as we all thought her folks were loaded. Her Dad owned a business and they lived in a huge house. Their cars were brand new, the drunk Mom was covered in gold and jewels and her father had the kind of expansive attitude that gave the impression of immense wealth.

Turned out her father was accused of having an affair with one of his employees, a girl whose responsibilities included paying employee taxes. Well, she didn't (so the story goes) and the IRS came after Betty's parents. They owed hundreds of thousands in back taxes and had no way to pay. They were irretrievably and utterly screwed. Everyone hated the obviously incompetent and lying female employee. Her sordid story about the Dad buying her lingerie and them meeting at hotels during the daytime, backed by reams of credit card receipts and physical documentation was completely discounted.

About this time, Betty's aunt died. Betty and her sister both inherited about 30k each. Betty ended up giving her parents all of it, in drips and drabs, over the course of about 6 months. They had no money coming in, so she basically supported them. The messed up part was that her parents were used to "living large", and wouldn't admit they were broke, so they kept spending Betty's money until it was all gone. Then they lost the house.

The whole time I kept telling her that she was throwing it away, but she said her parents just needed to get a few things going and they'd be fine, that they would pay her back. They never did.

We had been together about a year, and one night after swilling most of a bottle of cheap scotch, I said we should get married someday. Even though it was nearly 2:00am, Betty immediately called her twin sister, her parents, and everyone else in the world to tell them that I had proposed!

Wait. What just happened? No one holds anyone to a drunken rambling pseudo-proposal, right? I mean, we were just talking, right? Not anymore... I was stuck. I only had a few options. I could back out and pretend it was all a joke, delay it indefinitely, or I could move forward. Remember, she was still loads of fun so I thought, why not? I was 27, how long did I really want to wait? She's cool, she's as crazy as anyone I've known, and she's easy to be around, mostly because she does what she's told.

Yep. She did EXACTLY what she was told. She wasn't a slave, but she sure acted like one.

> "Betty, go do XYZ."
> "Great! On my way!"

This was another aspect of her personality that really rocked my world at first, but got old fast. Everyone says they want a girl like that, but live with it long enough and you'll realize, it sucks.

> Betty: "I believe XXXXXXX!"
> Me: "That makes no sense. Here's why: YYYYYYY."
> Betty: "You're right! I believe YYYYYYY!"

She would change her mind and enthusiastically support me no matter what. I used to test her by changing my mind on basic things just to see how far she'd go. I never reached her limits.

I weighed all this in my mind and figured, "Why not?" I'd never met anyone better, she was absolutely crazy about me, may as well marry her. I couldn't afford a ring and had to wait for my Student Loan disbursement. Yep. I was so stupid that I spent my student loan on an engagement ring. I still cringe at that.

We went out to a nice restaurant and I formally proposed. Sure, the first one had been a drunken one, but I was determined to do a real one too. She squealed as if it were the first time, gave me a big kiss and the entire restaurant clapped. I have to admit I liked the attention and I actually felt pretty noble.

Now came the moment I was dreading. It was time for her to meet MY parents. Betty was sort of like an amoeba – stimulus, response. She would blurt out exactly what was on her mind and I just knew she'd say the wrong thing at the wrong time and the weekend would be a disaster. I wanted my parents to approve of her but they are just so buttoned down and reserved. They were pretty much the exact counter to her family. My Dad was a preacher and didn't drink. My mom played the piano in the Church, my sister led the Choir and everyone was highly religious. I should have known things wouldn't go well, but I had to hope, right?

Initially, everything went better than expected. Betty was bouncy and happy and while my family might have had some reservations, they saw I was serious and they did their best to make her feel comfortable. Since everyone knew how tight my finances were, my sister said Betty could wear her wedding dress. I'd let them know on the sly that Betty's parents were in really difficult financial straits and any help they could give would be appreciated. This was nice in theory but horrible in practice.

My mom and sister took Betty into the back room so she could try it on and waited around to help her into it. Betty tried to say no, that she could do it alone, but they insisted. Well, she wasn't wearing any underwear. "Who cares?" you may ask. Well, as my family is hyper-conservative, so this freaked everyone out. What kind of girl doesn't wear underwear? Is that the kind of girl we want our precious snowflake to marry?

With the exception of the embarrassment with the dress, the rest of the weekend went well and afterwards I called my parents and asked them what they thought. They told me they thought Betty was very nice and that they just wanted me to be happy. This is "Southern-speak" for RUN!!!!!!!!

It was about this time she told me about her first orgasm coming from a dog. As I mentioned earlier, we were sitting on the couch watching the Dog Show when she blurted it out. I didn't know what to say. On the one hand, what the hell? But on the other hand, this was a woman I was supposed to marry. I'd met her parents. She had met mine. She had the ring. She had a dress. We had set a date.

So I asked for clarification. She said she was 13 or 14 and was sitting naked in her room when her dog came up to her sniffing around. He started licking, it felt good so she let him keep doing it, and then she came.

How do you respond to that? After my initial shock, I ran down my options for response and couldn't think of a single one that fit.

1. Did you return the favor?
2. Wow, that must have been ruff!
3. So that's how you train the dog?

I decided to shrug and say, "Wow, crazy" and go back to the show but I tended to look at our dog a bit suspiciously after that.

So, to summarize: I was now formally and fully engaged to a submissive torture-porn fan who required anal stimulation to come, who had nearly-bankrupt parents, a ghetto sister, a retarded brother, and a twin sister who, by now, I totally wanted to fuck. Betty wouldn't let me, by the way. Hey, I guess she did have a line she wouldn't cross!

We had a break from school and decided to take a road trip. I really wanted to see my old Army buddy Dirk and find out what he and his wife thought of my new fiancée. What better way than to rent a convertible Mustang, drive up to NY and spend a week with them?

The thing about Dirk was he was an utter dog. Everything I learned about women he taught me and in the Army we were legendary. We were the crazy guys who showed up to the Battalion Christmas party in togas and every time a new class of girls arrived after graduation from BASIC Training, they were immediately met and warned about us.

Dirk and Karin married in the Army and the three of us had been close for nearly 10 years. I valued their opinions more than those of my family, to be honest. My family knew me until I was 18 and left home so their impression of me was the guy who went to Bible College, not the guy who partied harder, drank more, and had more women than everyone else. I needed to know what Dirk and Karin thought.

We got up to NY and they loved her. Both Dirk and Karin thought she was the best girl I'd ever dated and told me to stop worrying and just marry her, her canine-history notwithstanding. They rarely liked the girls I'd presented, probably because the ones I liked the best were kind of bitchy, so for me to show up with a happy-go-lucky ball of energy was completely unexpected.

Betty liked them as well, especially Dirk, but not in a way I'd anticipated. I had told her that Dirk and I had multiple threesomes with women when we were in the Army, so I guess her little brain made the obvious leap I'd completely missed. She must have thought that I'd brought her up there to fulfill her fantasies with a good friend, someone I trusted.

The three of us went out one night and Betty and I thought it would be fun to have sex in the back of the car with the top down while Dirk drove down a windy road. Hey, why not? Sounds like fun, right? I'd never done it before and how often does the chance come up?

After a bit, we pulled off to the side of the road and Betty said, "So, is Dirk going to join us?"

Cue the scratched record sound. All of a sudden, three things hit me.

1. Betty thought this was all planned.
2. I was going to have to let my best friend fuck my fiancée.
3. After this trip, she wasn't going to be my fiancée anymore.

I could have said no, I suppose. At that point, it just didn't matter. There was this epiphany and I realized that I could never marry her. I wasn't the guy who could tie up his girl and let other guys have their way. What she needed I couldn't give her. I like to try everything and step through every door, but there comes a time when you just have to get off the train and that time had arrived.

We spent the rest of the week there, had a great time partying and drove back to South Carolina. I don't like to make quick decisions in areas of import, but things went downhill pretty quickly after that. She sensed something was wrong and tried to get me to just go to a Justice of the Peace and get a quickie marriage instead of going through the whole wedding thing. I guess she was worried I would leave and figured she should lock things down while I was still committed. Yeah, that wasn't happening. We started fighting about the wedding more and more and she finally laid down the ultimatum – if I didn't want to go down and get married, I probably wasn't serious about her. I said that as much as I cared about her, she was probably right and we should take a break and try to figure out what we both really wanted. This wasn't the answer she was expecting so she tossed the ring on the table and left.

Sweet mother of God, I was free! Our friends were stunned as I hadn't told them any of the things that were going on with us. They tried to convince me that she and I should get back together but that wasn't gonna happen. Our time together was over. This isn't to say we didn't hook up now and again – hey, she really was a demon in the sack, but it was for fun, not as a precursor to marriage.

Every time we'd hook up, Betty would update me on her family's situation. It turned out her drunk bimbo mom had divorced her Dad and moved on to greener pastures (i.e., someone with money). Her ghetto sister had shot and killed a guy who had tried to break into her apartment and although it was close for a while, the police eventually decided not to charge her.

The twin sister had broken up with my buddy and was dating some new guy named John I knew slightly through another buddy, Brian. Betty had dropped out of school and was working as a waitress. Although we were supposedly only hooking up for fun, I got the sense she was trying to keep the relationship going, maybe trying to get back together with me.

I knew there was zero chance of that happening and then it hit me... My friend Brian and John were also pretty good friends. Betty and her twin sister had dated best friends before, perhaps it was time for them to repeat the cycle. I called up Brian and asked him if he were interested in dating a really fun girl, John's girlfriend's twin sister. Why yes, yes he was.

Well, their blind date went extremely well and it wasn't long before the two of them were "inseparable". After that, my conscience was clear. Betty was happy, I was in the clear and I didn't have to worry that she was sitting around sad because I'd been a dick and dumped her.

I took a job up in Washington D.C. and remember getting the call that Betty and Brian were getting married. I was absolutely crushed. I knew I had engineered our breakup and my reasons were excellent but somehow... I knew she was wrong for me, but I couldn't help second guessing my decision. I wondered if maybe I should have done something differently, but finally came to the conclusion that you have to look forward, not back.

Life moves on and so did I. A few years later I met a great girl and proposed and this time alcohol wasn't involved. We were married at a beautiful ceremony in Sedona, AZ but had our reception at my parents' house in North Carolina. Betty and Brian drove up for the reception and they seemed happy, so I figured all's well that ends well. It was years before I'd see her again although we talked every now and again.

She had a few kids, I had a few kids and it seemed like her life had calmed down. One day I got a message from her saying that her email was changing and that she and Brian were separating. I fired off an instant email asking why. I mean, from what I could tell they were perfect together. He liked to tell her what to do, she liked to do what she was told and they had two very affectionate dogs.

Have you ever noticed that people never give you the real reason first? They always dump a pile of crap on you and if you sift through it, you can sometimes find the truth.

In her email she said she wasn't really fulfilled, that life wasn't what she expected, that Brian was controlling and another page or so of justifications, but the last sentence was the real reason. "I also realized *I liked women more than men.*"

Ah HA! Now the truth comes out. I gave her a call and pointed out that had she mentioned this earlier, we could have had all sorts of fun. She said she hadn't known herself and only recently realized it. Hey, whatever. Go, follow your dream. We only have one life and wasting it being someone you aren't is a recipe for misery. I wished her well and hung up.

SOME STORIES

About a month later, the other shoe dropped. I heard through the grapevine that Betty's twin was getting a divorce as well. Well, it made sense. What one twin did, the other had to do.

So now we have two divorced twins, one of whom is now dating a big fat woman. I've always wondered about that, by the way. If you're going to go over to play for the other team, wouldn't you upgrade? Just seems logical.

Fast forward another 6 months. I happened to be in the same state as Brian, so I dropped by to say "Hi". He was broken. You ever meet someone who is one dropped plate away from eating a bullet? That was Brian. He was living this kind of desperate routine where absolutely his whole life was devoted to his kids.

His back yard rivals Neverland, with tree houses (yes, multiple), swings, etc. He wants his kids to have fun every time they are there. I remember him being really funny, now he's just trying to get through the day without blowing his head off.

Anyway, he caught me up. Betty was no longer gay. I have to say, I didn't see this one coming. When she told me she was gay, it actually made sense. She was addicted to the Indigo Girls, loved flannel, took me to a lesbian book club meeting and had gay friends, so it wasn't too much of a stretch. For him to tell me that she wasn't gay was just crazy. I was blown away. This was less than a year after Betty decided she had to leave her family because she liked girls better, and now she's not gay? I asked him why, but of course, Brian was clueless. Their relationship was, at best, strained. And things were about to get even stranger.

He told me that the reason Betty's twin divorced her husband was that she decided that **she** was also gay. It turned out she had left her husband, John, for the very same woman that Betty had left Brian for! It couldn't be a coincidence! I never really believed the whole "twin bond" thing but with this information, how could I possibly deny it? Two twins left their husbands for Sally, a fat, ugly woman.

But that wasn't the end of the treasure trove of gossip from Brian. The bimbo drunk mom was now a widow. If you recall, after she left Betty's dad, she married an old boyfriend who had "made good". A few years after they married, he died unexpectedly and she inherited everything. In just a few years she went from married and broke to single and broke, to married and rich, to single and rich.

Of course, not having whatever wiles Betty's mother possessed, Betty's father was still broke. Maybe karma kicked his cheating ass, but for whatever reason he was nearly destitute and his ex-wife gold-digger bimbo was loaded. In fact, part of her inheritance is a really nice house at the lake. **Where Sally is now living.**

Yep. The girl who both twins "dated" is now living in the twins' mom's lake house and the twins live in Sally's house. Why? No clue. It makes no sense. By now I'd given up trying to understand them. Some things are best left unquestioned.

Last time I checked, Betty was straight and living with a new boyfriend, her twin is still living in Sally's house, and both John and Brian are husks of the men they used to be.

SOME STORIES

So I guess I dodged a bullet, or as one clever guy pointed out, "Dude, you didn't dodge a bullet. You're fucking Neo."

2. CHEATING AND WINNING A KISSING CONTEST

The job in D.C was fun, but my last year there I spent 362 days on the road and I was just burnt. I wasn't making enough money to matter and decided I was done. The client site was located in central New Jersey and I was sick of hotels, airports and conference calls. I knew if I saw another minibar or had to use another tiny bottle of shampoo I'd lose it. I decided life was too short to wear a suit and tie and told my boss I was done.

My Army buddies Dirk and Karin were only a few hours north of there and when I told them I was quitting they told me to bring my ass up there. They lived right outside of Woodstock and I figured it was as good a place as anywhere to land. I packed my car and drove north into my new life.

I love Woodstock. It's full of earthy hippies, tie dye shirts, and lots of crystals. Maybe the people there are stuck in the 60s but they're friendly and fun and if you get a contact high walking down the street, well, there are worse things in life.

SOME STORIES

Dirk and Karin lived in neighboring Saugerties, a sleepy little town with a few antique shops, quaint diners, mom-and-pop stores and an oddly out-of-place strip club. Dimly lit and straddling the city limits, the Ace of Clubs was short on class but never entertainment. I saw a mother drinking, cutting loose and cheering on the dancers absolutely lose her mind when her daughter unexpectedly came out on the stage.

People always say "There's no sex in the 'Champagne Room'" and it might be true. However, at the Ace of Clubs, I can personally attest that there's sex on the desk in the back office because I was nearly killed by that little paperweight thing with the nail that sticks up. I think it's called a desk spindle. Long story but take my advice and clear the desk before challenging a stripper to "show me what you got" after she's done a few rails.

I didn't discover the charms of the Ace of Clubs until months later so as far as I knew, the only fun was to be found in Woodstock or partying with my friends. Hey, not that there was anything wrong with that. I loved my friends and was looking forward to spending time with them. We had years of catching up to do! I didn't know it then, but that was all about to be put on hold.

About a week after I arrived, the town was all excited because the big event was happening! The Garlic Festival was coming to town! When I told people I'd never heard of it they looked at me like I'd never heard of Santa, or Jesus, or Oprah. Ok, ok, I'm a dumbass. Just tell me already.

They helpfully explained that every year, about 40,000 people show up to eat everything garlic. Garlic chocolate, garlic bread, garlic jam, etc., all are available and most are disgusting. A large part of the money in the town's coffers comes during that one week and the entire town gets into the spirit of the event. Stores redecorate, hotels rent rooms for triple the normal rate and during that week Saugerties is the only place in the country you're completely safe from Twilight fans.

Anyway, Dirk, Karin, and her extended family (to be described later) went every year, so they were all excited. I don't mean any disrespect to them – hey, I said the town was sleepy. Anyway, the big day arrived and everyone trooped down to help set up. This festival is such a big money-maker for Saugerties that everyone who actually lives there is expected to helps out.

I went down because I had nothing better to do, plus it's fun getting lit and watching people eat food that would make those crazy food channel guys vomit. Who the hell would expect garlic peanut butter?

Anyway, I got up early and drove down to the local high school where the annual event is held. Dirk, his wife and her family had already arrived and were sitting around drinking coffee and munching donuts.

Bear with me while I go through this, but it's important and you have to know who everyone was to fully appreciate how badly I screwed up.

Dirk married Karin. Karin's sister Leeza lived across the street. Leeza was married and has 5 kids. In addition, they lived next door to Karin's parents. So basically, you have the grandpa, grandma, 3 daughters, 1 son, 2 sons-in-law, 9 grandchildren, living within 200 feet of each other. Every weekend they'd get together and BBQ, they watched each other's kids, they went shopping together, etc. They were and remain a very tight clan.

Back to the Garlic Festival. The day wore on, it got warmer and warmer and the group moved from coffee to beer (in my case, Jim Beam and Coke). Everyone was having a blast and watching the crowd when this gorgeous young babe walked up. Everyone greeted her and introduced me. Turns out she was the girlfriend of Leeza's son Chad and had just turned 18. Well ain't that sweet. As we were hanging out watching the tourists gorge themselves on garlicky goodness, someone said they heard there was a kissing contest later that day.

Yeah, I get the humor of a kissing contest at a garlic festival, and it was put on by "Sweet Breath", the bad-breath drops people. The prize was $500 bucks, and who doesn't want that? In my half-lit state, an idea started to crystallize and after it formed, I started chuckling. I knew how to win. I said as much to the clan and they all wanted to know how.

I told them and said that I knew I could win, but the only problem was I didn't have a girl to do it with, since I'd only been there a week or so. Hot, newly-turned-18-year-old High School girl said, "I'll do it with you. I can use the money. It will be fun." I liked her instantly. Her attitude mirrored mine. Jump through every door right? Take every opportunity that presents itself and fun will ensue!

I would like to point out that at this time NO ONE OBJECTED! No one said, "War, that's a stupid idea, and you can't possibly think this will end well." Nope, everyone was all for it. Even stranger, no one seemed to think that Chad would object to my making out with his

18-year-old girlfriend. In fact, his mother gave me the prop I needed to win.

I couldn't believe my luck. I was about to make out with a Hottie, win 250 bucks, and my newly adopted family would think I was the coolest guy ever! What could go wrong?

Hottie and I decided we should probably practice, just so we didn't look awkward. I'm not going to lie. It was my idea. Sure, it's important to sell the idea but I was far more interested in the insanely hot girl straddling me and making out with me. We "practiced" for about an hour, and then we went to sign up.

People gave us all sorts of strange looks, since I was in my late 20's and this chick looked pretty young, but we were holding hands and smiling at each other so it had to be legit, right? RIGHT?

We signed up and all that was left to do was wait. There were only about 10 entries, which kind of surprised me, since 500 bucks is 500 bucks, but it just made my odds better. First couple up was a pair of geezers. Damn, damn, damn. Old people get the "awwwwwww" vote every time. The next couple up was a pair of really good looking people. The girl was stunning and the guy looked like he stepped out of the pages of GQ.

It looked like a movie kiss. The bastards were going to screw up my perfect plan! I knew we were going to have to be perfect to win and as we sat waiting for the rest of the contestants to try their best, I realized we had a fighting chance. No one else did anything special. It was finally our shot and I took a deep breath and we stepped up.

SOME STORIES

I held her and, pulled her to me and we began to kiss, slowly at first, then more passionately until all of a sudden, Hottie pulled back in shock. You could see the judges trying to figure out what had just happened. She reached up into her mouth and pulled out an engagement ring.

Yep. Genius. She looked at me, then the ring, then back at me, then her eyes lit up and I said, "From the moment I met you, I knew there was something special about you and I want to be with you forever. Will you marry me?"

Well, she was supposed to say yes and then kiss me, but she improvised and just devoured me. The judges lost their shit. The crowd lost their shit. People were cheering and for a second I forgot it was all a lie. She pulled back and one of the judges said, "Well? What did she say?"

Hottie said, "YES!!!!" Everyone cheered a bit more, patted me on the back, hugged her, and we walked away. We had a few hours to wait until the kiss-off (the judges had to select 3 finalists) and decided the best thing to do was to stay in character. Yep. More "practicing". I would like to point out that the ring that we used was donated by Chad's MOM! So no one had any reason to be mad at me. They were all in on it.

We went back for the kiss-off, but it was a done deal. The judges told everyone what had happened and everyone cheered us again, then they presented us with the check for $500 and told us that if we wanted to, we could get married in 1 year at the next Garlic Festival! I felt a little guilty that they were so nice, so we smiled, said thanks, and bolted.

THE WARLIZARD CHRONICLES

You know how you're watching a movie and then they start playing some minor chords to let you know that everything isn't really ok, that something bad is about to happen, and that the world as you know it is about to change? Yeah, I didn't hear any of those, but I should have.

That night, we all trooped over to Leeza's house and were eating dinner when her husband, AKA Chad's dad came home. Now he had been absent throughout the day and was a bit uptight, but tonight he was bouncing off the walls.

"Guys, you won't believe what happened at the Festival today! This guy proposed at the kissing contest by passing an engagement ring to the girl with his mouth!"

Utter silence. No one said a word.

He looked at all of us in confusion, then at his wife, who wouldn't meet his gaze, at her parents, who were examining the ceiling, then at me. I shrugged. You could see the wheels turning in his head. There was this look of understanding that dawned and then he said, "War?" We all continued to exercise our 5th amendment rights and finally he said, "Who was the girl?" His wife said softly, "Hottie."

So now, all the people who had cheered me on, provided me the props, and watched the whole thing go down threw me under the bus. See, there were a few things I didn't know.

Chad was this guy's pride and joy. My making out with the girlfriend wasn't cool with the father. Actually, that's a vast understatement. It was more like an unforgivable offense worthy of beheading. At least.

SOME STORIES

He was one of the main organizers of the garlic festival and they had already promoted this with the local paper. Hey, human interest story, right? Now he knew it was bullshit, it had happened with his son's girlfriend with some reprobate who had just arrived in town.

No one told Chad prior to this going down. I just assumed Hottie would have mentioned it to him, just to give him a heads-up, out of respect. Nope. I brought this up to her later when we were having sex and she just said she didn't know why she never called him.

So now I was the bad guy. Everyone started to backpedal wildly and say how they'd always thought it was a bad idea, how they'd had misgivings, and they were shocked, SHOCKED that I'd even think of doing such a horrible thing.

I pointed out that I'd even borrowed the ring from the Chad's mom, but no one wanted to hear it so I bounced. Dirk met me about 10 minutes later and said that everyone was pissed as hell at me but that he and Karin thought it was hilarious.

I knew we had to cash the check early, so Hottie met me the next morning and by 9:05 we each had our $250. The paper that day had a blurb about us, but they were working off of old info, so we were still cool.

The father went back, told everyone it was a fake, at which point everyone involved hated me. I'd obviously taken advantage of this poor girl, cheated the system, and didn't deserve the money, but since I'd already cashed the check, it was too late. Point of note: One judge said he was so impressed by my originality that he would have given me a higher score if he'd known at the time.

I was feeling pretty unloved, so when presented with the opportunity to further "practice" with the Hottie, I threw caution to the wind and went for it. We had a ton of fun, and then the Woodstock Times called and asked if they could do an interview with us. Sure, why not? Everyone hated me now anyway, I figured. I was wrong. For about a year after the article came out (front page, giant pic of the two of us) people would stop me and ask if I were the guy that cheated with the high school girl to win the kissing contest at the Garlic Festival.

Yes. Yes I was...

Epilogue

Right after this all went down, everyone was mad at her too. See, they all knew that they'd helped me, and although they had to be mad at me for family harmony, once things cooled down a bit, they knew that she bore an equal part of the blame. There was plenty of mad to go around. Chad was mad as hell since Hottie had embarrassed him and he was taking shit from all his friends, so he wasn't talking to her. The parents were furious, the grandparents were appalled, so who was left? That would be me...

I was sympathetic and understanding and she started coming over after work to hang with me. Remember, the whole family lived within 200' of my house so they saw her car there and saw it stay until around 2am. This did not endear me to them, but as I mentioned earlier, they were already mad, and she was ridiculously hot, so why not take advantage of the situation?

Up until this time, Hottie and I had just talked, but one day she came to me and asked me what I would do if I found out she were pregnant. See, that's the advantage of dating young girls. The extra years of experience help you out.

Sometimes I do things I'm not very proud of.

I said that I thought she was awesome and I could see myself with her for many years to come, that it wouldn't matter if she were pregnant from her 16-year-old boyfriend since we'd be together anyway. Let the sex commence!

See, I figured she thought she might be pregnant and thought she could seal the deal with me by throwing me a piece. I just had to say the right words. Which I did. But she was one of those girls who needs to feel like she isn't bad, that she kind of just fell into the situation and that it really isn't her fault. She was the exact opposite of Betty in this way.

Anyway, we started fooling around, things got hot and heavy, but she kept telling me that we shouldn't do it, that it was wrong, that cheating was wrong, etc. I have to tell you, this is really tiresome. At this point, my job was to provide her with some excuse, some rationale that would allow her to bang my brains out guilt-free but frankly, I was tired of playing games.

I like things to be clear and unambiguous so I told her that if she wanted to stop right now, we'd stop. I told her that if she just wanted to be friends, that was cool too. And then I told her if she wanted to fuck, that she needed to bite down on the heel of my hand and if she did, I would know that all the things she said were bullshit and that anything else she said going forward I'd ignore, no matter what.

She grabbed my hand and bit down on the heel hard. That was my answer. The rest of the night was her telling me that I was raping her as she had her legs wrapped around me pulling me in, that there was nothing she could do to stop me, and that she was a horrible person for cheating on her boyfriend. All of this happened on the front lawn, in clear view of her boyfriend's house, my house, and her boyfriend's grandparents' house. It was late, so we got away with it, and it was awesome.

Dirk finally approached me and told me that my actions were causing all sorts of trouble within the clan and I needed to knock it off if I wasn't serious about her. I denied that anything had happened, naturally, but that didn't matter. Hottie went back to Chad and high school and I moved on to greener pastures.

A year or so later she ended up being my maid and things picked up where they'd left off, but that's a story for another day.

3. HOW LSD GOT ME READY FOR WAR

Getting ready to go to war is like preparing for a big date, but instead of trying to get laid, the goal is to come back alive with all your limbs intact. The problem is, many people don't. Back in 1990 I was in the Army, stationed in Germany, working in Military Intelligence and the word came down that some General somewhere wanted to deploy M.I. assets to Iraq. Since we were all either German or Russian linguists, we failed to see how this would affect us. After all, there aren't too many Germans and Russians in Iraq, right? Right?

When we learned we were deploying, most of us lost our minds. We had heard about the projected estimates of 40,000 U.S. soldiers dead from chemical weapons, saw the pallets of body bags being loaded up and decided that if we had to go, we were going to do everything we ever wanted to before we left.

So we went nuts. To that end, we made lists of the things we wanted to do before we died and started doing them. Do you have a crush on someone? Tell her.

Hate the way your last relationship ended? Drunk dial her and confess your undying love. There were no virgins in our Company when we left. Anyone who hadn't had sex up until then hit the Red Light District and took care of that particular checkbox.

I did all those things and more, but the last thing I did before leaving was drop acid. I had heard about it all my life and figured if I was going to die choking on chemical weapons10,000 miles from home, I may as well try a little piece of paper with a tiny bit of chemicals on it first.

At first I was scared to buy it because I didn't want to lose my security clearance, but we all thought we were going to die anyway and the least of our worries was getting busted. To be honest, they stopped drug-testing us as soon as we found out we were deploying. I guess they wanted to make sure no one smoked a ton of weed to get out of going to Iraq.

Everybody knows someone who can score. For me, that was Sgt. Ramon. I gently let it be known that I was interested in trying something new and he came through. I also got a hit of MDMA (although we called it X back then), but the bastard ended up taking it himself so I didn't get to try that one. Anyway, I got enough for me and my friends, because we all wanted to see the Virgin Mary, or Jesus, or a flaming skull reciting Shakespeare. We really didn't know what was going to happen but it was cheap fun and we were ready. As the saying went, 5 will get you 8, and 5 bucks for 8 hours of a new experience is a good deal by anyone's standards.

So anyway, I was completely clueless and sat there looking at this tiny piece of paper wondering what the hell I was supposed to do with it. I'd heard something about putting it in my eye but Ramon said to just put it on my tongue and let it sit there until it dissolved. It did, but that was all. Nothing else happened. I figured the whole thing was a giant scam until I couldn't figure out why I had this stupid forced grin on my face.

We had made a pact to write down the experience on my computer as it happened so we'd have a record, but that didn't work out. The computer was entirely too confusing to operate and although we stared at it a while, it refused to read our thoughts. Stupid MS-DOS.

We all started grinding our teeth and since the computer wasn't working, we decided to head down to Sachsenhausen. "Sachs" is the greatest party spot I've ever been to. It's a two-block area right across the river from the Frankfurt zoo with 84 bars stacked 4 high. Every type of bar is there, from Irish Pubs to German Techno, to punk, to swing. If you were into something, there was a bar that catered to you. We spent most of our off-time there, picking up girls and getting lit, so when we realized we were tripping balls, we figured the best thing to do was to go someplace familiar.

This took about an hour. I didn't know then, but I know now, that your perception of time changes when you're on acid. Every little thing takes forever, or maybe it doesn't, but you have no idea what's real and what's perception. The reason it took so long to leave was the keys to the house were at our feet and no one could figure out how to get them. We stood in a circle, staring down at them and some indeterminate time later, it occurred to me that I could just pick them up.

THE WARLIZARD CHRONICLES

We clustered downstairs and somehow managed to make it to the train station and a couple minutes or hours later we were a few blocks away from some of my favorite bars in the world. Kailami's was a South African bar with a jungle theme. The seats were tiger-striped, the walls were woven wicker and there were pictures of snarling animals all over the walls.

In retrospect, going there was a poor choice. I was losing my shit and so was everyone else. We huddled in the corner, terrified and tripping our asses off. Snarling lions were looking at me, the wicker walls were writhing snakes and we were all barely holding on to some semblance of reality.

This lasted until our friends approached. We were such regulars that we tended to see the same people everywhere we went so the girls charged us, gave us big hugs and sat down to have a few drinks with us. They didn't know we were baked so they just started talking as if we were drunk, as we normally were. We did the best we could, but one girl finally asked me, "Why are you staring at me like that? Is something wrong with you?"

"Well, something isn't wrong with me, but I'm looking at your face and your eyes are spinning, your cheeks are drooping, and your nose is this giant pulsating blob."

She looked at me as if I were nuts and decided she had someplace better to be.

My buddy leaned over and asked if I had really seen that and I said I was just fucking with her. We sat there staring at each other and nodding gravely for another 15-20 minutes. After a bit, I guess he had finally taken all he could and he disappeared for about 7 hours. The rest of us lasted another hour or so and headed back to my apartment to see if we could get the computer to work. We couldn't.

About 2am there was a knock at my door. There stood my lost buddy, staring at me, saying nothing. He stood there looking at us for a couple minutes, or maybe an hour, then slowly turned around and walked away. Poor bastard.

The next day we all got back together to compare notes and decided although it had been interesting it wasn't something to do all the time. As an experience, it was worth it, but not as a lifestyle. We were about to experience enough horrible shit to last a lifetime, so chemically altering our brains to make things more exciting has far less allure than it used to.

Whatever the case, we shook hands and agreed to keep this experience to ourselves, went our separate ways and three weeks later we were in the Persian Gulf.

4. WAR

People ask me all the time what it's like to go to war and to be in combat. I usually tell them we played chess and drove around, no big deal. Maybe it's worth putting some of it down, just so if my son ever thinks about joining up he knows what it's like.

I was in Germany in a Military Intelligence unit assigned as a German Linguist. I'd learned German at the Defense Language Institute and after an additional 6 months of training, deployed to one of my favorite countries in the world. Germany is incredible. It's gorgeous. The people are fun, the food is amazing, and the girls don't think their breasts need to be hidden. That alone makes it worth visiting during the summer, but living there was one of the best times of my life.

Military Intelligence is filled with bright people who managed to hide enough of their past that they could get a security clearance. Mine was Top Secret, Sensitive Compartmented Information (although when I was in, it was "Special Compartmentalized Intelligence). TS/SCI clearances are granted to people who the Army believes are capable of and willing to keep their goddam mouths shut. The idea is that if you're in SIGINT (Signal Intelligence), you don't need to know what the guys in HUMINT (Human Intelligence) are doing, so they compartmentalize information and assign a code word to that group. For example (and this isn't a real word but you'll get the idea), we might classify something "Top Secret – Dog" to indicate it was viewable by people who were cleared for "Dog" information. We were a bunch of snarky kids who looked down on the rest of the Army guys as a bunch of dumb-ass ground pounders. I came to appreciate them much later.

Our job was to hang around the East German border and eavesdrop on their radio traffic and, using "direction finding", plot their location on a map. We would sit for hours, scanning through the radio spectrum and hoping to hear something fun. When we did, we'd alert our team leads and move on. Depending on what you heard, the person you told would change.

Something you probably don't know – every single person in my unit had the ability to get a message to the President within 15 minutes. It was called a "CRITIC". The idea is that if we were to hear something so significant that it could be an act of war, the President had to know quickly. So the CIA came up with the idea that if you labeled a message "CRITIC", it could get sent up to the President, bypassing the normal chain of command. As an example, if I had heard someone talking about a nuclear strike, I would send it up, mark it CRITIC, and it would go to the President. I never sent one personally, but knowing that you are only 15 minutes away from the leader of the Free World was a helluva piece of responsibility. Let's be real – if you were to do that on something that was bullshit, your career would be over. But you could.

Working in MI during the Cold War, even though it was at the end, was fascinating. That job ruined me for the rest of my life. You know how people are freaking out about Wikileaks now? "Good lord! Egad! Things aren't as they seem!" Yeah. I know. They never were. What was so strange is that the information we saw every day was so clearly false and we just didn't give a shit.

But I digress. Our Battalion was full of German and Russian linguists, Direction Finding equipment, Jammers (basically radio stations that sent out white noise and disabled enemy communications), and a company of badasses whose job it was to protect us. We knew our jobs were ending – what's the point of trying to sneak around and listen to radio transmissions when you could just walk over the border and take a picture of what was happening? The brass knew we were probably going to deactivate the unit and get split up, so they looked the other way while we spent most of our time sweeping the motor pool and getting drunk. We'd show up at formation at 7:30am, go play soccer, then shoot the shit for a few hours until lunch, which lasted 2 hours. After lunch, we'd screw around for another couple hours then go home. I had an amazing apartment across from Sachsenhausen, the bar district mentioned in a few of my stories. It would be fair to say I was drunk every night. We repeated that routine every day until some fuckwit named Saddam Hussein decided to invade Kuwait.

SOME STORIES

I'd never heard of the place, and frankly didn't give a shit. Why should I care? It's not like we would deploy, right? We were German and Russian linguists. What possible use would we be over there? All of our gear was cold weather; all of our equipment was painted green, brown, tan, and black. All of our camo was designed to shield us in forests. NO ONE IN IRAQ SPEAKS GERMAN OR RUSSIAN. All-in-all, sending our battalion would have been the stupidest thing anyone could think of. No one would waste Army resources in such a useless way.

I had forgotten that we were in Military Intelligence. Everyone knows that is the original contradiction of terms. So, just like clockwork, our orders came down that we were heading over. We learned this in October/November of 1990 and we were to deploy in early January. By this time, the propaganda machines were in full swing and we were all firmly convinced that Hussein was the new Hitler. I'm not arguing he wasn't a horrible person, but at the time we believed that one day, he just up and decided to attack Kuwait, a bunch of happy, peaceful, free-thinking freedom-loving people. When there is a gap in your knowledge, any information will fill it, so we believed this without question.

As our deployment date approached, the briefings started. They were mostly classified, but in some of them, they discussed what to do if we were captured. "Tell them everything", we were instructed. "As quickly as we're going to move, it won't matter." That made sense. We'd already done terrain studies and the place looked like a parking lot. "Oh, and they'll torture you using rats, metal bowls and blowtorches. So don't try to resist."

Wait. What?

Rats, metal bowls, and blowtorches? Yep. We were told that Hussein's troops would cut a hole in our stomachs, trap a rat in a metal bowl, put the rat/bowl upside down on our belly then, using a blowtorch, heat the metal bowl until the rat burrowed into our stomachs in defense. So they'd done a pretty good job of scaring us, but the worst part was that we clearly had no clue what we were doing.

The company commander had the Platoon Sergeants put together a list of things they thought the troops could use, including sunglasses, compasses, etc. Then he gave them a credit card and sent them to the PX to get supplies. They came back and distributed the loot out to use and we sat there in shock. They had purchased us kids' toys. The plastic wrist compass was "Suitable for ages 6+".

The entire build-up to the deployment was a series of mishaps, cluster-fucks, and occasional successes. The closer we came to our ship date, the better things started to run, until we were all ready. Well, almost ready. The worst part of all was coming up.

We were told to head to the gym about a week or so before our flight and when we got there, the walls were ringed with tables, but to get to them, we had to go through a gauntlet of guys with needle guns. Yep. Had to get the massive numbers of shots to supposedly keep us alive and free from disease so we could... I don't know, translate something? As I went from table to table, making sure all of my contact information was up to date, getting my bank accounts squared away and other administrative tasks, I got more and more irritated. It reached a head when I got to the table where I was told to make out a will.

This was where I finally broke. I refused. I said I didn't need one. They argued. I remained steadfast. They prodded and pushed, got my Platoon Sergeant, but I wouldn't do it. The line was backing up so they finally told me to keep moving, but they were pissed. I didn't care. I wasn't going to make a will because I would be coming back.

My final actions were to leave my apartment keys with a friend, kiss my girlfriend goodbye, get a really solid drunk on, and tell my German friends goodbye. That wasn't fun. My military friends, mostly the wives of guys in my company, were ok with the whole thing. Oh, they cried and said we should keep our heads down and our powder dry, but they "got it".

It was the German friends who were the worst. They didn't want me to go, couldn't understand why I was going, and looked at me with a combination of pity and disbelief. I tried to explain, failed, and said goodbye.

By now, we were ready. We had packed up our equipment and it was coming via boat, but they wanted us in Saudi so we flew out on a C-130. The first week of January we flew from Germany to Saudi Arabia holding our rucksacks, packed in like sardines, and facing each other. This sucked. We landed in Dhahran and headed over to a group of empty apartment buildings that we dubbed the MGM Grand. We still had no idea what our mission would be, so we sat around waiting for something to happen.

Out of boredom, we began practicing putting on and taking off our gas masks, and that's when one of our platoon members accidentally injected himself with atropine. Atropine injectors are spring loaded needles encased in a plastic tube. You jab the tip to your ass or thigh, the needle shoots into you and pumps you full of enough atropine to keep you going after a nerve agent attack. At least that's the theory. It's supposed to kick up your heart rate so when Specialist "Johnson" injected himself, his heart rate jacked up and he was taken to the hospital.

Of course, this was funny as hell to all of us. You see, Johnson was a special sort of soldier. He just wasn't all there. Every unit has at least one, and ours was Johnson. To give you an idea, when the word spread that someone had injected himself, the first question was, "Was it Johnson?" When they issued us bullets, he was the only troop not given any. Think about that… We were going into a combat zone, we all had full complements of bullets, except one person who was judged incompetent to carry them for fear he might shoot himself or someone else accidentally. With that said, Johnson spoke 5 or 6 languages fluently. He was still useful, just not if we were being shot at.

A little shy of two weeks, most of us headed out for 500 mile road march, to a place designated "Log Base Echo". We left some of our people behind at the port to receive our vehicles when they arrived, and they ended up getting hit pretty hard by SCUD missiles.

SOME STORIES

People always want to know why soldiers fight. I can't speak for everyone, but as soon as we got the reports in that our friends had been in the building the SCUDS hit, the point became moot. Those fuckers had attacked my family and they would pay. It's really that simple.

We were on the road march and I think it was after midnight on the 15th or 16th of January when we got the report that we had started bombing the Iraqi invaders. We were cheering like crazy, hoping that this would mean they would just turn around and go home, because then we would do the same. Plus, we wanted them dead and 6000 pound Daisy Cutter bombs tend to do that.

We could hear the bombing faintly in the distance, a constant rumbling, and although we knew that people were dying, we just didn't give a shit. We watched that night as flight after flight went over our heads, dropped their payloads, then came back and we wondered if the "war" would be over that night, or if it would take a couple days. I mean no one can withstand a constant bombing, right?

We reached Log Base Echo and set up our tents. We had driven about 500 miles, which really sucked, but we'd finally made it. As a quick aside, the way the Army moves is everyone gets in a column and drives the speed of the slowest vehicle. When the shortest-range vehicle is running low on gas, they stop, refuel everyone, then start up again. This means that if no one is low on gas, we didn't stop. There is no option of pulling over to pee or shit. You just keep moving. So we developed a way to pee while on the road. The camo poles were hollow tubes of aluminum about 3 feet long. We would take one, open the door to the Hummer slightly, poke the tube out, and pee through it. This was slightly nerve-wracking because if the end of the tube were to touch the ground, it would rip your dick off.

Fortunately, we all arrived safely, genitals intact. As far as shitting went, I don't know anyone who shit the first 2 weeks we were in country. All we ate was MREs (Meals, Ready to Eat) and it's all protein, so there was very little fat in our diet.

After we set up our tents, we were told to dig foxholes. On the list of things I hate doing and will never do again, digging foxholes is pretty high up on the list. First of all, it's morbid. Why do you dig a hole in which you can hide? Because someone is attacking you. Why are they attacking you? They want you dead. Great. So considering we wanted to remain alive, we pulled out the shovels and attempted to dig. Nope.

The ground was rocky and the shovels weren't even denting it. At the time, it was around 35 degrees so standing around digging a hole and failing miserably while not even knowing what our mission was going to be was pretty depressing. I wandered around until I found some ground that was softer and we dug there. Before long, we had a nice fighting position set up, big enough for two people to stand comfortably, and headed back to bed.

The guard duty roster was set up and we were told to get some sleep, since we'd have to "Stand To" at 3:45am. Um, what? Turned out there were reports of dismounted infantry in the area and to protect against a sneak attack, we had to be in our new foxholes, ready if they attacked at dawn.

What. The. Fuck.

Remember, we were kids who joined to have a bit of an adventure, get some college money, and were pretty much a bunch of pussies. So up until that time, we still thought that someone else was going to fight this war. We made sure our M-16A2s were in good working order, our ammo was packed tightly in the magazines, and we went to bed.

I had guard duty that night from 10pm-12am but since we were on complete light discipline (i.e., no lights of any kind, no smoking, no flashlights, no headlights, etc) we all just went to bed when it got dark. I did my guard duty, walking the perimeter, wondering how the fuck I'd gotten there. I began to get angrier and angrier at this fuck Hussein, the reason I was here, and it wasn't far to go from that anger to a hatred of all things Iraqi.

Dehumanizing the enemy is sort of Military 101. They aren't like us, they don't have feelings like us, they're pretty much animals who are trying to kill us, right? Later on, when our 1st Sergeant told us to shoot everyone who approached, no matter what, it was easy to accept, because by that time they weren't really people, they were just a threat.

The next morning, we got up in the freezing cold and huddled together quietly in our foxholes, waiting for an attack that didn't come. We did this the entire length of the air war, which lasted right around a month, every morning wondering if that were going to be the day we were attacked. During that time we built better foxholes, filled sandbags, put up triple-strand concertina wire, and picked up the vehicles that were too heavy to fly and had to be shipped in.

Life was actually pretty good until about 2 weeks after we arrived when our Nerve Agent Detectors went off. I'm not sure how much you know about nerve agents. Probably very little, so I'll give you a quick rundown. There are three types of chemical agents – nerve, blood, and blister agents. All of them can kill you, all of them are nasty, but the nerve agents are especially bad. Per Wikipedia:

"Poisoning by a nerve agent leads to contraction of pupils, profuse salivation, convulsions, involuntary urination and defecation and eventual death by asphyxiation as control is lost over respiratory muscles."

Fun, eh? We had special equipment that would alert us to the presence of one and with enough advance notice, we would be able to put on our chemical warfare (MOPP – Mission Oriented Protective Posture) gear. With enough time, you could get to MOPP-4, which meant you were wearing a full charcoal suit that would supposedly filter out the gas, gloves, boots, and a full face mask with hood. I was coming back from the chow tent with some hot food when someone screamed out, "GAS GAS GAS!!!!" Someone's detector had gone off. They have a range of about 3 miles, but we didn't know how close the attack was so everyone freaked.

I had my mask, since we always carried them with us, but the rest of my gear was back at my tent. Training kicked in and I dropped what I was carrying, put on my mask, cleared and sealed it, then ran back to my tent for the rest of the gear. If you've ever gone SCUBA diving, you know that breathing through a regulator is hard.

SOME STORIES

Amp that up a bit and you'll get a sense of what it's like to wear a gas mask. Every breath takes work and trying to shoot straight while wearing one is impossible without a ton of practice. Running in a mask is even harder.

We had spent 24 hours in full MOPP gear in Germany, just as a dry run and it was horrible, so I was hoping that this wouldn't be a repeat. I got to the tent, pulled out my gear and fuck me, it was wet. The effectiveness of MOPP gear degrades when wet, so I was out of breath, freaking out, desperately trying to get on my gear, and hoping I wasn't going to die a horrible death. You see, when you have a clearance, you get to see things that most people don't, like watching a goat die after being hit with nerve agent.

I didn't want to be the goat.

After a few hours, the 1st Sgt. called all-clear and we went back to cleaning our weapons and wondered what the hell had just happened. Had it been a false alarm? Had we been hit? Did our gear work? We had no idea. This theme ran through my whole time over there – we rarely had any idea what was happening. We still don't.

Our detectors went off another 6-8 times when I was there, not just in Saudi but in Iraq and Kuwait as well and we wrote it off as false alarms but now I wonder. We know he had the gas. We know he used the gas on his own people. A large number of my unit has been diagnosed with Gulf War Syndrome and some speculate that the gas might have had a role.

Another wonderful thing you have to understand is that soldiers are guinea pigs. As soon as we arrived at Log Base Echo, our squad leaders were issued pills and we were told to take them. They were called NAPP pills and they said that if we were to take them, we would be better off if we were hit by gas. Our squad leader walked down the line and watched each of us take them. What were they? No idea. Were they tested? No idea. How did they work? No idea. Take them and shut the fuck up, Soldier. The Army thinks it's good for you, so take them.

Of course now we know they are linked to Gulf War Syndrome but back then, we weren't given a choice. We just took them. Some friends in different squads were just handed them and told to take them. They didn't. No one who wasn't specifically forced to take them did. I wish I'd been in a different squad.

It was about this time that I first pointed a weapon at someone. We had another report of bad guys in the area and were told to go check it out. Early on, the squad leader had asked if anyone wanted to be the M-60 gunner and I'd volunteered. I didn't care that it was heavy and a pain to carry. I figured I'd always prefer to be the best armed person around and the M-60 is portable death. 200 round box of ammo, belt fed, tracer every 6 rounds, all you have to do is pull the trigger and whatever you hit is dead.

We'd jury-rigged a mount for the '60 on the top of the Hummer, so I was up top and we pulled up to a truck that had broken down about 10 clicks from our base. We didn't know why they were there, so we went in with maximum caution. When we got there, it was one old guy and about 5 women. The women were covered head to toe in the traditional Muslim garb so all we could see was their eyes. The really bizarre part is

SOME STORIES

that they kept re-arranging the part that covered their mouths. Our squad leader was talking to the guy and they kept looking at us, taking off the lower part of their veil enough so we could see them smiling at us, then they'd put it back on. All of them did this. I don't know what they were doing, but it felt like they were flashing their tits at us.

After about a month of bombing we were told we were going into Iraq. By this time, we were sick to death of sitting around and welcomed the chance to go destroy the people who'd made our lives such a living hell.

I couldn't wait…

You know, this is getting a bit grim and the actual war stories are hard to write. I think it's time to take a break and get back to some funny stories.

5. THE FRENCH GIRL

So one of the few times I did acid, I was in Germany and some friends of mine and I ended up at a little place called "Jazz Life" in Sachsenhausen, a crazy bar district in Frankfurt. This place was off the hook. It was the greatest place on Earth, like Disneyland for adults.

Anyway, we ended up at Jazz Life and I was baked out of my gourd. I remember meeting some girls and chatting them up as best I could. I was on the downside of my trip, but I was lucid enough to set a date with one of them for the following evening's party at a buddy's house.

The following day came and I was trying to make sense of the previous night. I knew I had a date but couldn't remember what she looked like, so I asked my buddy who hadn't been tripping. He told me that the girl was an utter hound, that she had a gigantic nose and that under NO circumstances should I keep the date.

Well damn. I remembered having a pretty fun time with her, but my pride wouldn't allow me to show up with a date to a party with an ugly girl, so I avoided my house until after the party. When I got back the next day, there was a note taped to the door. I don't have much in the way of shame, but this note made me feel really badly.

This girl had waited for me to show up for a couple hours, **in the rain**, and I never showed. She said that if I wanted to see her, to meet her back at Jazz Life on Sunday. I figured that since I was so mean I had to make it up to her and there was no way I could blow her off twice.

The next day I went to Jazz Life, figuring I'd just suck it up, make some excuses, and leave, but holy hell there she was, cute as hell! Turned out my buddy was talking about her friend! I lied my ass off, said I was so sad that I'd missed her and was so glad she was willing to give me a 2nd chance.

We dated for the next few months and I learned I was deploying to the Gulf. She promised she'd wait for me, there were lots of tears, and I flew off to the Persian Gulf. Now here's the part I'm not so proud of.

You know how you have the first few months of a relationship and they are just perfect, then reality sets in and things just suck? Well, I thought that if *she* thought I died, she could have the perfect relationship forever, that nothing would ever mar it, or break it, and her memory of those few months would remain unblemished.

So I never responded to any of her letters. Nothing. Not a single sentence. I never saw her again.

6. THE MARRIED GIRL

Ok. This was in Germany and is one of the many things I'm not especially proud of…

There was this girl who lived in the apartment building, a few floors down. I don't know why, but she took a bit of a liking to me and kinda hovered around. She was married to a gigantic infantry guy who was as nice as he could be. She was … at best, lumpy. She wasn't exactly fat, but she had this look of bovine confusion that made me want to disappear every time she came to bring me cookies, or whatever. I dunno, she was just … dull.

Anyway, one night my friends and I were watching one of my favorite movies, "Henry V", the one with Kenneth Branagh. We'd been drinking and "Sharon" showed up. Actually, I have no idea what her name was, but this will do. Anyway, my buds had been mocking me about her for a long time, so she showed up with more cookies, which she handed out, they gave me the look of schadenfreud, and left me alone with her. I had already had most of a bottle of vodka (the cheap shit, not Goose), and I just wanted her to go.

I had a cookie, of course, since her cookies were heavenly, and she sat there making small talk. I replied as politely as possible, trying to get her to leave, but then she asked me if I wanted a massage. Well fuck. Who doesn't want a massage? So I was getting a nice massage when she told me that it would be better if I took off my shirt. I did so, oblivious as fuck. After a bit, she said gleefully, "My turn!"

Well fuck me. I should have seen that one coming. No one gives a free massage. I thought quickly, or as quickly as I could as drunk as I was and said, "Ok, but you have to get naked first." Now, bear with me... I figured she'd storm out. Hey, she was married right? She was just flirting, right? Well, she stripped down faster than I could have imagined. Oh hell. Now I have a naked annoying lumpy girl standing in front of me because I told her to get that way. My options were twofold:

1. Gracefully decline.

2. Man up and be polite.

I figured I'd get away with the naked massage, but she wasn't having any of that. Her back was like one of those memory foam mattresses that conforms to your spine and gives you a perfect night of sleep and when my fingers sunk in I started frantically wracking my brain for a graceful exit.

Then she started massaging back. One hand reached back between my legs to return the favor and all of a sudden I thought, well, she isn't exactly hot, but I certainly don't want to be rude. What kind of man would ask a woman to get naked and then leave her hanging? She could really have her feelings hurt to get rejected after she put herself out there and showed me her vulnerability.

The horny male's ability to justify himself and rationalize truly horrible behavior is second to none. Add in the vast quantities of vodka I'd already consumed and I was finished. I stopped thinking about how unattractive she was and started focusing on how enthusiastically she was going to town on me. There really wasn't any way I could stop now without insulting the lady and what kind of gentleman would I be if I were to do that?

Folks, I did my duty. I decided if I were going to cross that line I would give her the best I had to offer. While it's true I was wrecked, I was also attentive, inventive, and did my best to give her the finest lay of her life. There was no way I was going to be able to finish myself off, as drunk as I was, but in a further display of absolute selflessness, I faked a massive orgasm (yep, the one and only time) and told her how awesome she was. Quick side-note – every girl wants to think she's the finest to ever hit a mattress and it never hurts to tell her she's right. Of course, there was no way I was going to go for a repeat, so I told her that she was awesome but that she was married, both of us were clearly carried away by the moment and we could never do it again.

A few days later her infantry husband came up knocking on my door. Now I'm 6' and was in pretty good shape, but this guy was a monster. He basically told me that it was making him sad (huh? *SAD?*) that his wife was coming up to my place all the time and that although he knew she'd never do anything, it just didn't look good. I agreed with him on all counts and said that she just knew I was lonely and was being a good neighbor. He thanked me and left. She never came up to my place again, but she used to wink at me in the hall.

I still think I did the right thing in the end. I know it was stupid and I got myself into the situation, but once I was there, I did my duty. She had fun and as I always say, you should try everything at least once.

7. THE ARREST

I'm writing these stories as I think of them and so there's no real order. This one's a pretty good one but I want to tell you 100%, don't do this at home... Seriously.

This happened back in the summer of '95 when I was in college, right after Betty and I had broken up. I'd moved into an apartment right across the street from the Humanities Building in Columbia, SC, mostly for convenience since all my classes were less than 5 minutes away.

Since I was right on the street, most of the time I'd just hang out in the front yard, having a drink and talking to other college kids walking by. After a while of this, I got used to the casual atmosphere and it was common for people I'd never met to stop to have a drink or just to shoot the shit.

One day, this guy stopped by and asked if he could borrow some butter (yeah, I know, I was also initially suspicious too). He said he and his girlfriend were making a cake or something and needed a stick if I could spare one. He looked like your standard long-haired hippie type, and at the time, so did I. I hadn't shaved since I got out of the Army, hadn't had a haircut, and due to my poor laundry skills, was wearing what looked to be a tie-dyed shirt.

We started bullshitting, he saw my hang-gliding certificate, we talked about rock-climbing, but the odd coincidence was that I sort of knew his girlfriend. Back when I lived with Betty, there was a guy who lived upstairs from me who made low-budget horror films. Well, I was in one of them because it was partially filmed in my house, but turned out that this guy's girlfriend was the main lead! Small world.

Anyway, Spencer (Real name. Fuck him.) and Shannon (Also real name.) lived two doors down and so we ended up having a drink and chilling out for a bit. A few bourbons later, he drops this on me: "Hey man, you know anyone who could use some C-4?"

WTF? This was a few months after the Oklahoma City bombing and an Army buddy of mine was slightly wounded in it so I was more than shocked that some fucking hippie stoner had C-4. I didn't say anything for a bit, then casually said that although I didn't need any, I could ask around. He left with a stick of butter and I got out the phone book. First number — FBI. Answering machine. 2nd Number — ATF. Answering machine. Well fuck me. It was the weekend and everyone had gone home, I guessed.

At the time I was working in a little computer store and one of our customers was a local police Detective, so the next day I called him and told him what had happened. He told me he'd get me in touch with the right people and the next day I got a call from S.L.E.D., the State Law Enforcement Division. Unfortunately, Spencer was at my house at the time, so I answered vaguely and they gave me a number to call back.

I told Spencer that I was going to a gun show that weekend and that I planned on talking to the guys there, since they were pretty hardcore and I was sure someone would want it. He bolted and I called SLED back. We set up a time to meet and I headed out, full of pride in my civic duty. What a fucking dumbass.

I met with the SLED guy and told him what had gone down. They grilled me for about an hour and I told them every detail I could think of, then they asked me if I would be willing to wear a wire and get this guy off the street. HELL YEAH I would! How cool would that be? I was so enthusiastic that they finally mentioned they knew this guy and that he had a conviction for armed robbery. At this point, I should have known they weren't playing me straight. They waited until I had already said I'd do it to tell me an incredibly important part of the story, that this guy was dangerous. Oh, I wasn't worried at all. I was a combat vet and some fucking hippie didn't scare me.

So I called up my parents and told them what I was doing, how I was going to wear a wire and bust a bad guy. They were so proud, how wonderful I was to step up, etc, etc, blah blah blah. A few days later, I talked to Spencer again and set up the buy.

I told him I had met a backwoods survivalist at the gun show who was all into machine guns and shit and he wanted to buy both bricks. Yeah, the stupid motherfucker had two bricks. If you don't know, one brick a bit larger than a deck of cards will obliterate a car. We set the price at $1000 and the buy for the next evening at my house.

Next day dawns and I was humming like an engine at 10000 RPM. I was a "Confidential Informant" who was taking down a bad guy. Oh, and even getting paid!

My detective buddy had told me that the SLED guys would compensate me and that I may as well make a few hundred off the deal. I resisted at first, since I wanted my motives unquestioned, but I had a bunch of parking tickets that my previous roommate had racked up and I needed the money, so I swallowed my pride and talked to the SLED agent. I said I wasn't looking for money but that I wanted my parking tickets to go away. Hey, I was helping them out, they could help me out. They ended up giving me $300 bucks to clear the tickets since it was easier than trying to work with a judge. Hey, it was all good. In retrospect, I think this may have changed their opinion of me. Not sure.

Anyway, the big day comes, and it's time to get wired up! I thought they'd put it in my crotch, or around my stomach or something, but they ended up putting it around my right bicep, between my arm and ribs. Three agencies were involved — SLED, the city police, and the university police. We went over the plan which was as follows:

1. Spencer shows up at my house.

2. SLED agent shows up at my house.

3. Spencer shows off his C-4.

4. SLED guy says, "That's some good C-4 there" and good guys bust in.

5. Bad guy goes to jail for 5 years or more (that's what they told me, at least) and I bask in knowledge of a job well done. Go ME!

Yeah. As they used to say in the Army, a plan is only good up until the first shot is fired. Anyway, the first few steps worked out. Spencer showed up, we had a drink waiting on the SLED agent, then he showed up.

Spencer tried to be all cool, but in the end, he pulled out a piece of white putty about the size of a marble and gave it to the SLED agent. The agent looked at it, then put it into my ash tray and lit it with a lighter. It burned white hot and was completely consumed. I couldn't help it and asked, "So? Is it C-4?" He said, "Yep. That's definitely
C-4."

Fuck me.

The cops listening heard something that sounded close enough to the code phrase and busted in. We were handcuffed face-down on the floor and just stayed silent. Spencer, fucking rocket-scientist that he was said, "Dammit, Shannon told me this was a bad idea." Good job Shannon. Now she's complicit. The cops went over to his place and fortunately found the two bricks, so Spencer and Shannon were hauled off to jail. The cops all congratulated me on my bravery and for doing my duty, all of which I modestly took and then they left.

GO ME! How cool was that? In the next few days, I heard that they'd found the guy who had given the stuff to him and it was some dumb Army kid who needed money, so it wasn't a big conspiracy, but even so, maybe I stopped someone from killing innocent civilians. That's good, right? I paid off my parking tickets and things went back to normal.

Almost.

A few weeks later, I was in my favorite bar and a guy I kinda knew came up to me and told me that some guy named "Spencer" was looking for me, that I had ratted him out and that he was pretty pissed. I shrugged and told him I had no idea.

WHAT THE MOTHERFUCK?

I called up the SLED agent and said, "What the fuck is Spencer doing out of jail, let alone looking for me?" His response was beautiful and completely destroyed any illusions I'd had about the cops.

"I'll talk to him," he said. "Keeping quiet was a condition of his release."

Turned out that to get him to turn over his source, they told Spencer I'd turned him in. Then they turned him loose. So this convicted armed robber who had tried to sell high explosive was back out on the streets the NEXT WEEK. Nice job, justice system.

The SLED agent promised to call Spencer and get him off my back, but by now I was really questioning my decision to help these rat-fucks at all. A few days later, I was back in the bar and same guy came up to me again and said, "Dude, Spencer is still looking for you. He's pissed that you turned him in and even MORE pissed you ran to the cops and tattled."

Well fuck me. So apparently the influence of the police wasn't enough to keep this asshole away from me. At this point, there was really only one option left.

"Ok, here's the deal. You tell Spencer that if I ever hear anything about this again, I'll kill him. If I see him again, I'll kill him. If someone comes up to me and says Spencer's looking for me, I'll kill him. I'm armed and no one will give a shit about some dead felon, but they will give me a fucking medal. I'm a goddam combat vet and the last thing in the world I'm going to worry about is some dumbass hippie who wants to kick my ass."

Yeah, big words. I never heard from Spencer again. I also moved about a week later. Fuck that. I'm not going to sit in my living room and wonder if every person walking by has a shotgun. Of course, I broke my lease, and my landlord sued me. My lawyer landlord. My local lawyer landlord. So I went to court, told the judge the whole thing and he said that although there were mitigating circumstances, there was nothing he could do. Boom. Judgment for over $7000 against me.

So doing my duty cost me my apartment, a $7000+ judgment, and I looked over my shoulder until I left the state but hey…

At least I paid off my parking tickets.

SOME STORIES

8. MY COWORKERS PRANK ME GOOD

I was asked, what's the best prank ever played on you? Here is the answer.

This was years ago, but we were moving our office from one location to another one about 200 miles away, and we were all a bit keyed up. No one really wanted to move, but hey, you have to do what your boss says, right? Anyway, we're driving down the road and traffic was NUTS. Long line of cars, shitty day, gray, rainy, and we all just wanted this move to be over. Driving conditions were horrible. The road might as well have been unpaved there were so many holes in it.

Aside from the shitty road, the precipitation was so bad that people were pulling off to the side of the road to get away from it, looking for shelter anywhere they could find it. The weather got even worse, it got dark, and all I could think was how much this job WASN'T paying me... But hey, you make a commitment, you follow it. At least that's the way I was raised.

We had decided to just press through and not stop, figuring the sooner we got to our destination the better and stopping would just make things worse. I don't know if this was a good call but hey, hindsight is 20/20, right? Our car was pretty beat up by now but we figured hell, it's a company car, so fuck 'em. We just wanted to be done with this and head home.

So I'm sitting up on the top of the car, watching everything going on around me and all of a sudden there was a tremendous explosion behind me. I nearly shit myself. I mean, it was loud as hell prior to that, but this was so close I thought I was dead. I turned around and there was a huge cloud of smoke and flame coming from a tank about 50 meters away. I yelled, "Incoming", reasonably figuring they'd ranged us, when my buddies started busting up. Turns out the combat engineers were destroying Iraqi tanks, MID-BATTLE, and my co-workers knew, but since I was on air-guard and couldn't hear, they thought it was funny to not tell me.

9. Leaving DLI

Ok, so this was back when I was at the Defense Language Institute in California, while I was in the Army. I knew I was leaving the next day and I was pretty irritated because I'd just met a new girl and we had really hit it off. We decided we'd be boyfriend/girlfriend for another 12 hours, then we'd have a messy breakup and I'd leave.

We had a few more drinks and decided just being bf/gf wasn't enough, so we'd get engaged and then have a messy breakup in 11 hours. That turned into actually getting married, so we decided to have a fake marriage there in the barracks complete with bridesmaids and groomsmen, then have a messy divorce in 10 hours.

By now we were both pretty lit. My buddy Esteban performed the ceremony, I kissed the bride, and we went back to my room to consummate the marriage. Except she wouldn't do it. WTF? I couldn't believe it. For some reason, she just wouldn't have sex.

I was pissed as hell, since this was my only shot, and told her that instead of waiting another 9 hours, we could just divorce now. She stormed off in a huff and I said fuck it, got a book, and went out into the hall to smoke a cig.

After about 10 minutes, I saw a set of legs walk by, but didn't look up. They went by again, then again, then finally stopped. I looked up and there was a blond chick standing in front of me. I was pretty lit, so I'll just say she was a stunning beauty. Yeah, let's go with that. Anyway, we got to talking and about 30 minutes later were up on the balcony of the Spanish department on one of the tables. 5 minutes later, we were going at it like mad. I left about 7 hours later and the last time I heard from her she sent a nice card to my new duty station.

Now that's class.

10. THE GERMAN REDLIGHT DISTRICT

When Army guys arrive in Germany, they can't wait to taste the exceptional food, visit the beautiful castles, drive 150mph on the autobahns and soak up the local history. Their interest in the rich cultural heritage extends beyond the atrocities committed during WWII and … nah, just kidding. They want to visit the Red-light District. Since most people in the States will never see it, I thought it might be kind of fun to tell you what it's all about.

The Frankfurt Red-light District is conveniently located about 3 blocks from the main train station on a street named Kaiserstrasse. It's open 24 hours a day and is generally clean, well lit, and makes the city a ton of money through taxes. It's also a hotbed of drug sales and other nefarious deeds, so visitors are cautioned to stay on the main avenue and avoid the seedy side streets.

There are different types of brothels, but the most common are called "Eros Centers" and are in apartment buildings. The girls are usually independent contractors who rent the room by the day and keep whatever they make. Unlike the girls on the street, they don't necessarily have pimps and are pretty shrewd businesswomen. There is an order and hierarchy to the girls and it's fascinating.

As far as I know, there's nothing official written down – it's just organized by demand. It may be the lower floor apartments cost more and therefore the highest earners are able to afford them. Anyway, here's the breakdown.

- First Floor – Playboy quality white girls.
- Second Floor – Penthouse quality white girls, Playboy quality Asian and Hispanic.
- Third Floor – Hustler quality white girls, Penthouse quality Asian and Hispanic, Playboy quality black girls.
- Fourth Floor – Skank white, Hustler Asian and Hispanic, Penthouse black
- Fifth floor – Junkie white, Skank Asian and Hispanic, Hustler Black
- Sixth Floor – All fat/junkie black girls and most don't require a condom.

I'm not sure if the 6th floor is considered hell, but it's the worst level and it's bad. Maybe it's where old black hookers go to die. Regardless, the whole place is fascinating, but I found it even more interesting that the racial mix was so clearly separated. People are so open and proud of their lack of prejudice until it comes to getting laid. There's a reason the first floor is all white girls.

SOME STORIES

The other piece of the puzzle was pricing and it was also floor related. The price came from the activity and the duration. Each time you went up a floor, the girls allowed you to do more for less and extended the time.

The best "bang for the buck" was the 3rd Floor. Sex with a gorgeous Asian girl for a half an hour was about $35 or 50 DM (Deutschmarks – this was prior to the Euro). Of course, there were guys in my company who blew their entire paychecks down there, and some never went above the first floor. One buddy of mine dropped $2000 in one night on one girl. This was the equivalent of 2 months of Army pay and we railed him for that one. Shit, I bet he's still paying off that credit card.

Legalized prostitution changes the bar dynamic wildly. In the U.S., if you want to walk up to a girl, you pretty much better buy her a drink. It's the price of admission and shows her a few things:

1. You're solvent and can afford her.
2. You're interested enough to put your money where your mouth is.
3. You know the rules of the game.

You can easily spend a whole night buying drinks and have her walk away after she gives you a fake phone number. This activity isn't discouraged, in fact girls won't even pretend to talk to you sometimes – they'll just take the drink and walk away with your mini-dowry.

It works because the girls have the power. They control whether or not you have sex. If you think the hottie you've been chatting up all night is going to bang your brains out, sure, have a few drinks! Hey, maybe if I buy her a few more her inhibitions will drop and she'll do me! By the time you're done, you're broke, drunk, lonely and horny.

Let's contrast that with living in Germany. Let's say it's 1:00 am and you're half-lit. You've been talking to some American girl for a while, maybe she's interested, maybe she isn't, but she wants you to keep buying her drinks and you're not sure where the whole thing is going. You look at your watch and decide that rather than chance it and waste the rest of your money on hopes and dreams, you're going to get a nice, hot girl who won't play games. You'll knock one out, go home, and fall asleep happy and well-laid for the price of a few drinks.

It's even more fun when the girl is German. She knows the deal, knows you don't need her to get laid and that a prettier girl with a better body is about 10 minutes away by taxi. She also has a completely different view of sex and isn't burdened by the American Puritan Ethic.

So now, instead of holding sex over your head, she has to prove that she's worthy in other ways, just like you have to do for her! I'm not saying that there aren't any stuck-up bitches in Germany. Of course there are. But on average, I think the relationships are healthier and more fun.

As mentioned earlier, new guys who have just arrived in-country are always fascinated and want to see the brothels immediately, but it's far more fun to get them drunk first.

SOME STORIES

Bravado is party of the Army culture and a subsection of that is how much you can drink. I know, it's stupid, but if you can drink a ton and still function, you have bragging rights and are free to mock the guy who gets wrecked off of a single beer.

These guys would arrive from the States and brag they could down an entire case of beer, so German beer would be nothing to them. Yeah. Let's put that to the test. As a quick aside, some of the most alcoholic beer in the world comes from Germany. Some of it is more potent than vodka. But sure, "newly-arrived-18-year-old", you can drink a case…

A few hours later we've proven our point, the new guy is sloppy drunk and insisting he's ready to go see some ladies! We'd take up a collection, head over to the Redlight and guide our drunk and cocky friend directly up to the 6th floor.

We would shove him inside, hand the girl 50DM, tell her that condoms were required then wait. A few minutes later, he'd come out with a big smile on his face, we'd take a picture of the two of them together, and the next day we'd post copies of the pic everywhere.

Everyone in the unit would know. It's hard to come into a new unit with a chip on your shoulder and a tough-guy attitude when a picture of you slobbering on a 6th floor girl is being passed around. Hey, humility is good for all of us, right?

11. ALWAYS BUY THE TICKET!

If there were a single theme to all my stories, it's that I took every opportunity that was presented to me. This is the story of a time when getting off my ass led to one of the greatest experiences of my life.

My buddy "Chad" sat down across from me at the chow hall and said, "Let's go to East Germany tonight."

The fact he was able to say that still blows me away and probably requires some background. My whole life growing up, we thought the Russians were going to attack us. We weren't sure whether it would be a ground assault like in the movie "Red Dawn" or if they were just going to fire a ton of nukes at us but we were all sure it would happen.

Magazines ran articles about the "Arms Race" and listed how many tanks, missiles, and troops we had compared to the Soviet Army. Heart-breaking stories about courageous Russian pilots defecting with their MiGs peppered every paper in the country. Every time someone made it out of a communist country into a free one, we cheered. We heard constant stories of how horrible it was to live without freedom, to wait in line for bread, to be restricted to where you could travel and to live in constant fear of the secret police.

After World War II, Germany was split in two, and became the battleground between the two superpowers. Each side was furiously spying on the other, trying to figure out what the other was doing, using wiretaps, double agents, moles, you name it. In the meantime, people were taking every opportunity to escape to the West, whether by tunnel, hidden compartments, or even by homemade hot-air balloons.

Every time another daring escape succeeded, we were reminded of those that hadn't and shown pictures of the bodies caught up in the barbed wire on the border. I guess the reason I'm going into such detail is that I hope you can imagine how it must have felt to have someone say, "Let's go to East Germany tonight", after years of people literally dying to get out. We weren't even allowed to visit there without special permission from the military because of our top-secret clearances and now my buddy was saying we should just hop on the train and head over, that we didn't even need passports or anything.

I had spent two years in training, learning German, memorizing East German military structure, listening to countless radio intercepts, and preparing for the war we all knew would come. I'd done joint exercises with the German and Dutch military, cross training so we could learn as much from our allies as possible. We had gone through lengthy classes on how to avoid becoming compromised by East German agents.

"Let's go to East Germany tonight."

How could I say no?

October 2nd, 1990, my buddies and I bought train tickets to Erfurt. We picked this city because it was a major military center and we had several weeks of classified school devoted to its role in the presumed upcoming war. I was pretty broke, so I grabbed the only alcohol I had, a full bottle of Bailey's Irish Cream and headed to our train.

The train looked just like you'd expect from the movies. There were separate compartments with sliding doors and as we walked down to our seats, through the windows in the doors we could see that the rest of the people in the train were also drinking, probably from much earlier in the afternoon. The mood was exuberant and infectious.

As mind-boggling as the concept of reunification was for me, it was a million times more so for the West Germans. Their whole lives they'd viewed the East Germans as the people who they were going to have to fight. I'm not going to go into WHY they reunified – it's interesting but long.

The important thing to know is that the West Germans had been afraid of the East German military for decades and that fear was suddenly gone. The East Germans were revealed to be just like the West Germans and couldn't wait to be part of a free country.

To understand the mood of the West Germans, imagine you're about to get an "F" in a class and the punishment is death, then you find out you're going to get an "A" and a party will be thrown in your honor. Now magnify that by a million. That was the mood on the train and up until that day I'd never seen so many people so happy.

As Americans in Germany, we faced prejudice daily from people who resented our presence. Not everyone was rude to us, but at least once a day someone would swear at us in German, not knowing we spoke the language. We never said anything – we just let it slide.

That night, there was nothing but love from everyone. It was a welcome change, so we, like everyone else, walked up and down the car, talking to everyone and asking what they thought of the reunification.

I poked my head in one car, repeated my question, one of the guys inside saw my bottle of Bailey's and his face lit up. It turned out he and his friends were all fans, so we joined them, traded shots from our respective bottles and within an hour were thick as thieves.

When we crossed the border into East Germany everyone cheered and soon after we pulled into the train station in a border town named Eisenach. Our new German friends got ready to disembark and we decided that as lit as we were, one East German town was as good as any other and we may as well hang with our friends.

What a depressing fucking place. Crossing the border was like leaving Oz and returning to Kansas. The buildings were old and run down, the cars were models I hadn't seen in years, the people were dressed in drab clothes but you know what? They were happy. No, they were beyond happy, they were joyous and as we soon as we got off the train we were enveloped by a crowd of people hugging us, crying, and slapping our backs.

We didn't look like Germans, and we were speaking English, so people knew we were probably American. They wanted to meet us, to shake our hands, and to see the people they'd feared their whole lives. They pulled us to a nearby club, started buying us drinks and trying to speak to us in broken English.

As it grew closer to midnight, people started heading to the town square and the bars locked their doors. Everyone in the square was drunk as hell, arms locked, singing over and over again, "Deutschland, Deutschland, Deutschland, Deutschland." Tears were streaming down faces everywhere, unnoticed and the look of disbelief on some of the older faces was heart-wrenching. For more than 40 years, these people had lived under the tight control of an oppressive regime. After tonight, there was no chance of it ever returning.

We counted down together as if we were in Times Square on New Year's Eve and when we hit "ONE!" a roar went up from the crowd, louder than anything I'd ever heard. At 12:00:00 AM, October 3rd, 1990, East Germany ceased to be a political entity and there was one Germany, for the first time since World War II. I was there to see it, not because I was lucky, not because it was an accident, but because I got off my ass and bought the ticket. That's my life. I always buy the ticket.

12. The "Spread"sheet

When I joined the Army at 20, I was a virgin. I'd only had a couple shots at changing that status, but passed because I thought I should be pure until marriage. Growing up in the church will do that to you, but as soon as I was completely out of the house, I started to re-examine what I believed, and one of the first things tenets I abandoned was the whole "no sex before marriage" thing.

It didn't take long – actually less than a month, before I made the jump. To be honest, she made the move, or it probably wouldn't have happened, but when a girl says, "I'm hot" and takes off her clothes, you pretty much have to man up.

At the time I was living in Monterey, CA, one of the most beautiful places on earth. Some buddies and I had a long weekend and decided to head down to Pismo Beach to celebrate. We filled the car with cheap booze, drove a few hours south and commenced to getting wrecked. There were a couple of girls hanging out in the hotel hot tub and we hit it off.

After a few drinks, things got hot and heavy. I ended up with the slender blonde Lori and my buddy Biff ended up with the curvy Christy. We couldn't do too much as we were in public, but we made plans to meet them at their house the next night.

The next day was spent hung-over as hell and that night we couldn't decide if we wanted to meet the girls or not. We had a killer party going on at the hotel and there were tons of people there. Fortunately for me, Lori showed up, grabbed us and took us back to their house. Why didn't both girls show? Turned out Christy was babysitting. I think it's important to stress here they were both legal in the state of California. Barely.

We all had a few drinks and after a bit Lori asked if I'd like to see Christy's brother's room. Well shit, I guess I would! The kids were sleeping so we snuck back and left my buddy and Christy to their devices.

I was so inexperienced. I really had no idea what to do when she took off her clothes but figured the best thing to do was to copy her. We made out for a while and the rest of the clothes came off. Well goddamit, it was game time and I still didn't have a plan. Fortunately, I'd read Penthouse Letters and if memory served, the best thing to do was to dive down below and not come up for air until 30 minutes had passed. Why 30 minutes? It was in one of the Penthouse stories and I actually thought that was normal.

There was a clock behind her head, so 30 minutes later, tongue exhausted, I moved up, wrapped my rascal and started poking away with all the skill of a blind fencer. I was unsuccessful. No matter what I did, I couldn't seem to get "Tab A" into "Slot B". Fuck. I felt like an asshole and figured a bit of lubricant couldn't hurt.

I told her to hold on a sec, threw on some boxers and walked out into the living room where the other two were going at it hot and heavy. They flipped out, thinking I was the kids, and looked at me like I was crazy when they realized who it was. I looked at them calmly, still drunk and said, "I know this is going to sound strange, but do you have any Vaseline?" My buddy Biff burst out laughing and Christy said, "Um, I think there's some in the boys' room, but they're sleeping." Yeah, sleeping kids weren't going to stop me. I snuck in, grabbed the jar and headed back into where Laurie was waiting.

1 minute later I was going at it like a champ, but the strange thing was that instead of thinking about how awesome it felt, all I could think was that I was finally actually having sex. After all those years of telling the girls I was dating that we had to wait, I was losing it to some girl I'd known less than 24 hours.

Important safety tip: Vaseline destroys the integrity of latex condoms. Just saying. They **will** break.

We finished the weekend with the girls and headed back. I was a new man, walking with a new purpose. See, the thing that occurred to me was that every girl that I walked by had a pussy. I know how stupid my epiphany sounds, how obvious it must be to you, but there is a huge difference between theory and reality.

In theory, they all could have sex but in reality, they could all have sex with ME! So that's what I did. I had sex with every single girl I could. I went nuts. If the girl was even marginally cute, I'd sleep with her. I did the

30 minute thing on all of them, thinking that was what I was supposed to do and they responded well. In fact, they'd recommend me to their friends.

I didn't get clingy – I was just there for fun and told them so up front. Because I worked so hard to make sure they enjoyed themselves, the word spread. By the way, I know I sound like a douche, but my goal was to make sure they all had at least one orgasm before we even started penetration. I had girls I barely knew asking me to check out their rooms, and next thing I knew I was getting laid again! This was the best thing ever!

Since I was a computer guy even back then, I started keeping a list of the girls I'd had sex with, what we did, how enthusiastic they were, etc. My buddy Biff knew about it but very few other people did. I figured if everyone knew, the supply would dry up. It was ok that Biff knew, since he was in the Marine Corps and didn't have the same friends. Plus, he'd talk me up to the girls he knew, and I'd do the same for him. One day we were at the chow hall (the cafeteria for you non-military types) and he introduced me to "Terri". She was skinny, 17, and exuded sexuality. I have always liked the skinny ones and she was hot as hell. My girlfriends couldn't stand her. I heard stories about the fights she had with her roommates over her indiscretions. It seemed she had a habit of jacking guys off and on more than one occasion her roommate flipped because she got tired of cleaning cum splatters off the wall.

So basically, she was perfect for me. She liked sex and came on really strong. There was just one minor problem. She was dating a friend of Biff's, this gigantic

SOME STORIES

Marine. Seriously, the dude was a beast. I felt a bit badly, so I pushed off and decided that I really shouldn't break the guy code, i.e., I didn't want him to kill me. Unfortunately, she didn't share the same thought process and had it in her mind that we were going to fuck, come hell or high water. I was semi-seeing someone at the time. Ok, I was chasing someone else at the time. That girl, whose name eludes me, was leaving the next day and I knew the window of opportunity was closing fast. The next day I was down grabbing breakfast and Terri laid it out. We were going to skip breakfast, go back to her room, and fuck.

There was nothing to be done. We headed back to her room, went at it, had a fun time, and I bolted. A few hours later I was in the other girl's room, saying goodbye, had sex with her, and felt like a champ! That was the first time I had two girls the same day. Remember, just a few months before I'd been a virgin, convinced that pre-marital sex would send me to hell. Now I was a heat-seeking sex addict. I made sure I put it all in my spreadsheet, partially to keep a record, but even more to somehow make real the fact that I was actually having sex with all these girls. Biff thought it was funny as hell. He was far more experienced than I was, but what I lacked in longevity I made up for in variety.

About a week later, Biff was up in my room with a few of my friends and, like nearly every night we were drinking. I forget why I had to leave the room, but I did and when I came back he and some friends of his had my spreadsheet up and were going through it. I didn't think much of it, as most of the guys there were high-fiving me. All of a sudden, a chill gripped me. The beast boyfriend of Terri was looking at my spreadsheet and I knew I was fucked.

He cocked his head, looked confused, looked at Biff, looked at me, looked back at the spreadsheet and then just crumpled. Ok, now I felt like a complete dick. I didn't know he actually liked her. Turned out he was in love with her. Everyone left and I sat there swilling Jim Beam and wondering how I was going to get out of this one. He was well within his rights to kick my ass. Fuck fuck fuck. The next day he came to see me. FUCK FUCK FUCK.

I talked my ass off. I said I had no idea she was anything other than a fuck buddy, that I thought it was all just fun, and that I was really sorry, that I didn't mean to hurt him. His man-gene kicked in and he decided that I hadn't been the one to wrong him, that Terri was the whore and I'd just been having fun. Holy shit, he bought it? Actually, she kinda did jump me. Yeah! It was all HER fault! The mind is a funny thing and it wasn't long before I was completely convinced I was the victim.

Self-delusion is a motherfucker.

So to summarize, I had sex with a monster's sexpot girlfriend and she got blamed. Oh well. I kept that spreadsheet for years, but finally stopped when I couldn't remember the people on it. I may have overdone it a bit, but oh well. I had fun.

SOME STORIES

13. I LOSE

Back in the late 90's, I was doing pretty well for myself. I had a good job, got to travel, wore suits and thought I was pretty cool. I was working at one of the Big 6 consulting firms and we were a bunch of arrogant assholes. Competition was fierce between the guys I worked with.

Armani suits, cashmere overcoats, and expensive drinks were all part of the image, but even more important that that was how hot your girlfriend was. I hadn't been in D.C. long and word came down that our Christmas party was going to be a huge blowout. I knew then and there, I needed to show up with someone ridiculously hot or I was screwed. The problem was, I didn't have anyone to bring. I was wracking my brain and considering going to a bar and bringing the best looking girl who'd accept, when opportunity knocked.

I was downstairs at the café, sitting outside and drinking coffee, trying to figure out what to do when, in the distance, I saw a gorgeous babe coming toward me. As she grew closer, I realized it was a girl I'd known in college but had never hooked up with. I'd been with "Betty" at college, so I'd never had the chance to pursue this one, and I'd always regretted it. She was slender, elegant, intelligent, world traveled, and if I could score her, I knew I'd win. Shallow? Sure, but then again, so was I. I sat there quietly, grinning, and waited for her to walk by. "Vanessa" walked up, glanced at me, did a double take and squealed "WAR!" She threw her arms around me, gave me a great big hug, and we spent the next hour getting caught up. Turns out she was living in D.C. now and looking for a job. She was recently single so I suggested we get together that weekend to have a few drinks. We met up, had a good time and made plans to see each other again. I played it cool over the next few weeks, didn't make any moves, just hung out with her when it was convenient.

One day when we were having lunch, I asked her if she'd like to join me for a black-tie party, that I thought we might have fun. I didn't tell her the full scope of the event, just that it should be pretty fancy and she'd need to dress up. Here's what I didn't tell her:

Back in the late 90s, computer consulting firms were making billions. Traditional companies were worried they'd get left behind, so they paid outrageous hourly rates to have someone come in and tell them how to retool with the latest technology. They looked at it as cheap, because the alternative was to lose their competitive edge to some new company that didn't have their overhead. With all that money coming in, our firm decided they were going to go all the way and show the world how successful we were. Through the grapevine I heard "The Ball" was costing the firm 2 million dollars.

SOME STORIES

Say that to yourself... The company spent TWO MILLION DOLLARS ON THE CHRISTMAS PARTY! It gets worse. They had offices all over the country and each major city had a similar ball. So they spent 2 million on the D.C. ball, not on all the balls around the country. I bet they spent 25 million that Christmas.

Vanessa agreed, said she thought it would be a great time, and that she'd go get an appropriate dress. I told her I'd pick her up that Saturday about 8. I was going to show her the time of her life, so I got a stretch limo, a really nice tuxedo, flowers, the whole nine yards.

Saturday came and I made sure the limo was well-stocked with vodka, wine, coke, water, etc. Vanessa flipped when she walked out and saw the limo. I was looking dashing, she was gorgeous, and I had the limo driver drive around D.C. to set the mood. If you've never been driven around one of the most amazing cities in the country, down the Potomac, around the monuments, I highly recommend it. The stage was set...

We pulled up to the convention center and I waited for the driver to let us out, just to make things a bit classier. The theme of the night was Under the Sea, and as this remains the most insane ball I've ever been to, let me take a second to describe it.

We had four large ballrooms, each with an open bar and a different type of band. One was rock, one was swing, one was pop, and one was reggae. Each had more food than anyone could imagine, all of it was fantastic, but what set this night apart was the actors and actresses walking around. There were pirates, mermaids, sea captains, deckhands, and the place was expertly decorated to give the sense of actually being underwater. There was one table filled with shrimp, a bunch of fish dishes, and various types of salad, but when we got to the shrimp, there was a mermaid sitting on a throne on the table. We looked up at her and she pointed to the shrimp and said, "It's ok, they weren't friends of mine."

Vanessa was having the time of her life. She was grinning ear to ear, hanging on my arm, and I could see the looks of the other guys. She was far and away the best looking girl there and I could see the looks of jealousy on my co-workers faces. Oh yeah, it was awesome. We danced until late that night, drank too much, and had an absolute blast. Stuffed, half-lit, and happy, we grabbed our gift-baskets and stumbled back out to the limo. Here I made my first tactical mistake. Instead of making a move, I dropped her off at her house, kissed her goodnight, and went home. Why? I don't know. I really don't know. What the hell was I thinking? I guess I was in "gentleman" mode or something, but honestly, it was just stupid. After a night like that, I should have stayed with her, just to enjoy coming down and talking about the party. I was a dumbass, I guess.

I was out of town the next few weeks and had to go to San Francisco for a conference, so I figured I'd make up for missing my clear opportunity. I called her up and asked if she wanted to meet me in San Francisco for the weekend. I was flying in from Chicago, she would be coming from D.C., and I booked the flights so we'd arrive within about 30 minutes of each other.

She flipped, said she'd love to join me, and I resolved I wouldn't screw this opportunity up. We would be in San Francisco, one of the most romantic cities in the country, just the two of us, and I would seal the deal. Nothing would stop me this time. Nothing.

The gods love to punish pride. I got sick as hell a few days before the flight and was coughing and sneezing, felt like death, but dammit, I was going through with it. I should have immediately gone to the doctor but figured it was just a little cold and I'd get better. We met in San Fran at the airport and she looked a bit shocked. I must have looked horrible, but I was determined. I rented a car and we headed to our hotel (separate rooms – I wasn't going to be presumptuous). I hoped some sleep would help me out, so I loaded up on Nyquil and went to bed, abandoning her to her own devices. I let her borrow the car so she wasn't stuck there, but I couldn't join her. She was a bit irritated, but resolved to make the best of it and headed out.

The next morning, I was even worse, but I couldn't give up. I thought it might be fun to head to Santa Cruz, where I'd spent a bunch of time when I was a kid. We walked on the beach, she looked gorgeous, I could barely stand up straight, and I realized I needed a wing man or this whole trip was going to be shot. My best friend from 4th grade lived there, so I called him up and sent out a distress signal.

We met at his parents' house, they took one look at me and said they were taking me to the hospital. Well fuck. My good buddy said he'd be glad to look after Vanessa for me while I was getting better and I gratefully and obliviously thanked him.

You already know where this is going. Hindsight is a motherfucker. I spent the next two days in the hospital with pneumonia while Vanessa and my buddy hit it off, took my rented car, went to wineries, watched the sun set over the Pacific ocean, and eventually ended up in my hotel room (I had the bigger one, naturally). She flew back and I got better but by the time I returned to D.C., she'd gotten a job and had moved. The worst part is my buddy later told me that she liked me but thought I wasn't interested because I never made a move.

So what did I learn from this? You never give up an opportunity because you never know what the future might hold. Oh, and when you start to get sick, go to the doctor

14. Learn to Shoot Pool.

There are certain things all guys should know how to do. You need to be able to hammer a nail without bending it, shoot straight, drive safely, but above all you damn well better be able to shoot pool. Why pool? I have met more people, made more money, and received more free drinks shooting pool than any other bar endeavor. I have played since I was young, but I didn't shoot seriously until I joined the Army. My best friend was a god and taught me how to shoot for leave, how to play with English, how bar pool strategy differed from tournament pool, and most importantly, how to impress girls. The first rule of picking up girls, according to The Tao of Steve, is to "Be excellent in her presence". In a bar, you have very little time to show the girls you're good mating material, so you need to have a hook.

Mine was pool. It doesn't matter how loud the music is, if you can run the table with style, you get noticed. Looks are great, but if you can smile at a girl and drain the 8-ball without looking, you score points that can't be made any other way. Plus, you fuck with her boyfriend's mind.

I remember one girl who was just blown away by my game. I trounced her boyfriend so badly that he was left with all his balls on the table and the game was over. I played it cool and said that I really had fun and I'd like to buy the both of them a drink. 20 minutes later, he was gone and I was fucking his girlfriend in the bathroom. Classy? Not at all, but it sure was fun. She turned out to be a bit of a nut. Her dad was a senior officer with the FBI and after a few weeks she disappeared. A month later, she showed up again, now clean and sober after a stint in rehab for her coke addiction. Oops…

Being able to shoot pool means no matter where you go, if there's a table, you'll meet people and have fun. Hell, just a few weeks ago, I was bored and ended up in a hipster bar in Columbus, OH. I was 15 years older than most of the people there, but within an hour I had an audience and a bunch of new friends. Pool does that.

It's important to note that being good is possible for anyone. It just takes practice. I wasn't naturally good, but I worked my ass off and practiced like crazy. I bought video tapes, did the drills, shot the same shot 100 times in a row, anything that would prepare me for the night in the bar where I could shine.

I've always been ridiculously competitive. I hate losing, like everyone, I guess, but unlike many people I've met, I bust my ass to prepare myself to win. I used to get to the bar early, shoot 10 or so games, get a nice buzz going on, then wait for someone to put their quarters on the table.

SOME STORIES

In a bar, people always want to shoot pool, so there are a few different ways to get on the table. You can write your name on the little chalkboard and watch people cross their names off as they play, you can put a quarter on the table and make sure no one takes it, or you can just wing it. Regardless of the method, like lambs to the slaughter they came. I'd hold the pool table all night, frustrating people who showed up late and had to wait an hour to play.

My finest moment was shooting a girl who'd waited 2 hours to play. She was kind of a bitch and made a big fuss about how long she'd waited, how bored she was, how the bar should really buy more tables, and by the time it was her turn, everyone thoroughly hated her. She racked, I broke the 8, which, if you don't play pool, means that the 8-ball went down on the break and she had lost.

She bitched and complained, so the people in the line let her re-rack. I broke the 8 again. She lost her shit. By now, people were so pissed at her they just wanted her to shut up, so they let her rack a third game. I ran the table. I broke, a few balls went down and I never missed.

This means that in three games, she never shot and lost 3 times. She was pissed as hell, but everyone told her she'd had 3 chances and that was all she was getting. She walked away mad as hell and the people around the pool table broke out in applause. Let's get back to the story…

In college, although I was working 3 jobs, I was always broke as hell. I pretty much supported "Betty" and was going to school fulltime, so I was always looking for a source of extra cash. My roommate told me that there was a tournament that Wednesday that few people knew about but paid out $125 cash to the winner. Holy shit! I know it might not seem like much now, but back in the 90s, $125 was a pretty good chunk of cash. Plus, if I could win it by doing something I loved, so much the better!

Wednesday night came and my roommate drove me to the bar. It took about 5 seconds for me to realize something was off. The bar was packed, but there were no women. Ok, I guess that kind of made sense, it was a pool tournament, but even so, NO girls? Not one?

When I saw two guys kissing I figured out why. Yep. Gay bar. This didn't bother me and it occurred to me that this could work to my advantage. I was a good pool player, maybe even very good, but in the Venn diagram of life, the intersection between good pool players and gay guys was pretty slim. My roommate and I were the only straight guys there.

I figured I would win easily, but I was wrong. It turns out being liberal and tolerant in theory isn't the same as having a guy in a crotch-hammock slinging his junk around on the bar behind you. I fucked up my first few games and only won because my opponents were distracted by the bar-boy. After a bit, I was in the finals and I managed to win.

Everyone was really cool, shook my hand, told me they hoped I'd be there next week, and paid me. WOOHOO! I was $120 bucks richer (winnings minus the entry fee) and I'd had a blast. I went back every week until they decided that I was no longer welcome. I think I won 8 straight (no pun intended) tournaments before they booted me. Oh, they were nice about it, but the message was clear. The tournament was for their patrons to have fun and they didn't like a ringer coming in and taking their money.

Shooting pool has always been the best way for me to meet people in bars. Look, if you're standing against a wall, sipping your drink and alone, the assumption is going to be that you're a loser. Think about it -- when a girl sees you by yourself, what's her motivation to talk to you? Are you so clearly awesome that she can't help herself and has to rush over to meet you? It's much more realistic that you'll be dismissed as a lonely creeper. I mean, you're all by yourself, how awesome can you be, right?

But if you're at the pool table kicking ass, you're someone who's there for a purpose. Sure, you might be there alone, but it doesn't matter. Plus, and this is key, you are physically incapable of paying a girl too much attention if you're also shooting pool. Just when she starts to get into one of her riveting cat stories, you have to shoot again!

Now she's stuck wanting to finish her story, but you're not available. I know this sounds stupid, but it works. Girls can't stand not having you hang on their every word and it drives them nuts. The best part is having everyone tell you how awesome you are in front of them too.

It's simple, we're all driven by our biology. Women want the dominant guy. I've seen girls ignore spectacularly good looking guys who should be models after I've dominated them on the pool table. It's really funny to watch. Cocky guy gets up to table. His hair is in place, his clothes are perfect, one eyebrow is cocked and the girls are all focused on him. He goes down to shoot and scratches. You sink 2-3 balls, maybe with a bit of draw so it looks cool. He misses. You drop a few more. He drops 1, but is stuck behind another ball. You knock down the rest and win. Good looking guy feels like a dork and his confidence evaporates with every missed shot. Girls can sense when a guy feels like a failure – it's a stench they grow to recognize very early on. Now you're standing there, having just obliterated someone who just a few minutes before was Mr. Awesome. But now he's pissed and feeling like a dork.

It's even more satisfying when you beat someone famous. Good looking guys are a dime a dozen, but when someone who is really well-known walks up and you blow them out of the water, it's an indescribably good feeling. When I was living in NY, my favorite place to hang was a bar in Woodstock called "The Pinecrest". Woodstock is famous for the music festival, but it's always been an artsy-type town and there are a bunch of recording studios there. Famous musicians go there to record their albums and like many of us, they like to grab a drink and relax after a long day.

Unfortunately for them, most of the places to have a drink are clubs. If you've spent a whole day recording music, the last thing you want is to hear is more music, so they would end up at the Pinecrest. It was just a simple bar with a pool table and I loved it. Rustic, fireplace, everyone was relaxed and it was one of my favorite bars in the world.

I was the best pool player in the bar, by far. It wasn't even close. People would groan when I walked in, bought me drinks to get me too drunk to shoot, and always wanted to be my partner. One night I was shooting especially well but this one shaggy-haired guy just wouldn't give up. He came back again and again, with different partners, alone, over and over and just couldn't beat me. We shook hands, he shook his head and left in disgust. One of the locals came over and asked, "Do you know who those guys were?"

"Nope. Not a clue."

"That was Phish."

"Who?"

"Goddam War, seriously?"

"What do you want? I've never heard of them."

That happened more times than I can count. Most of the time, the locals would wait until the game was over to tell me who I'd just beaten. The most satisfying was Uma Thurman's brother. He was a cocky bastard. I really enjoyed destroying him. I guess when your sister is a world-famous actress the sense of fame and entitlement rubs off.

I've shot pool on three continents, won a ton of money, been given countless free drinks, and made friends everywhere I've been because I was a good shooter. Hey, maybe you're rich, good looking, and own a bar so this is all wasted advice. But for the rest of you – learn to shoot pool.

BAD ADVICE

15. GO OUT AND LIVE

I logged into Reddit one day to see this post:

"DAE (Does Anyone Else) feel like they are just "killing time" every single day?
Like you are killing time, waiting for something to happen, but don't know what that something is and it ends up just being going to sleep?"

I hate this attitude and this was my response:

No. Every single fucking day I wake up like a goddam bull, ready to charge out and destroy everything in my path. Maybe I'll start a new business, maybe I'll buy a house, maybe I'll get in my car and drive to Texas, I don't fucking know, but I'm going to do something that makes me happy. Sure, I used to be sad and pathetic like you, not sure what I wanted to do with my life, until I realized, there is no "single thing".

I want everything. I want thick juicy steaks still dripping blood, I want wide-open blue skies, endless summer, ice cold glacier water out of the skull of my enemy. I want to fuck until I scream, drive up the face of a cliff, ride horses in France, blow 10 grand on peanut butter or maybe just buy the biggest suite in the place and sit around ordering pay-per-view. It's your goddam life you spineless fuck, no one is going to live it for you.

You better wake the fuck up now, or you're going to turn around, look at your Chrysler Minivan, your mortgage, your pot-belly and your thinning hair and wonder with crushing regret where it all went, how you got here, and what the fuck do you do now? Goddam, I want to slap you and wake you the fuck up. You want to know what to do? LEAVE THE FUCKING HOUSE and go explore. Fuck a midget. Create a stand-up routine and do open mike night. Yeah, you aren't funny. Get over it. Learn something new. Go out and live.

Then again, there is something to be said for a nice nap.

16. "That's Not Fair"

People complaining sets me off. It's a hot-button for me. I see so many people wasting their lives and sitting around bitching when all they have to do is just leave the room and go have adventures. People tell me, "That's not fair. Just because you did it doesn't mean that other people can." Huh? Actually, yes, you can. Everyone can.

What about the married ones working dead-end jobs and who have a bunch of kids? Yep, them too. There are just so many different avenues to try, so many places to go. All we have to do is just do it, but people are crippled by their fear of failure, by the prospect of parental disapproval, by lack of funds that the day they leave high school they begin to die. Think of it this way: Life is like one of those movies where the good guy is given poison and only has 24 hours to live.

If you knew you had 24 hours left, would you sit around and bitch about how everything sucked? Fuck no. You'd get up off your dumb ass and make those final 24 hours count.

BAD ADVICE

So that's all I'm saying. Kids are so used to being coddled by their teachers, by their parents, by ultra-sensitive therapists who want them to self-actualize that when they spew this bullshit, I generally smack 'em upside the head, not to be mean, but to get their attention.

I've found I can't be miserable and bored if I'm angry. ☺

17. I Really Like This Girl But She's Out of My League

The sad truth is that you're right. There are many girls out there WAY out of your league. They're too pretty, too smart, too rich, too funny, and why the hell would that want you anyway? I mean, you really don't have much to offer, so no point in even bothering. I mean, realistically just talking to them is going to end in rejection, and that's painful and embarrassing. You are kinda chunky, you have that one crooked tooth, your hair is thinning, and you tend to stare at your feet a lot. You'd better just hide in your room.

Then again if Lyle Lovett got Julia Roberts…

18. KEEP YOUR MOUTH SHUT, OR THE VIRTUE OF DISCRETION

Example: "Did you have sex with her!??!?!?"
Answer: "No."

It's always no. Suspicion is one thing, certainty is another. If you screw up and cheat, don't lay that on the other person. You move on, you break up, you leave, whatever, but you don't fuck them up for the rest of their life because you are a dick.

Let's say you're away at school and you pocket-dial your girlfriend while you're out with another girl. She might think something's going on, but she doesn't *know* there's something going on.

If she isn't important enough to you to keep you from having sex with another girl, break up with her. But don't tell her that while she was home thinking about you and missing you that you banged someone else. You break up like a man, you tell her that you're going different directions, but you stress, and I mean fucking vehemently stress that she's awesome and you would never cheat on her. Never.

Time goes on, she moves on, and she thinks to herself that she was probably just being silly, that she's awesome, that no one would cheat on her, and she's happy.

Or, you come clean, tell her yeah, you met someone and sorry. Now she's stuck with that in her head and every relationship from then on out, she's wondering... Is this guy as bad as you? Is he going to cheat? She starts asking too many questions of the guys she's dating and they leave because she's just too jealous. Her life devolves into a spiral of mistrust and it's all because you couldn't keep your mouth shut.

19. QUICK TECH SUPPORT TIP

I hate calling tech support. You end up talking to someone barely comprehensible guy named "Bob" who tells you to unplug your computer and plug it back in. I'm not 90 years old, "Bob". I know how to reboot my computer.

I used to get mad.

Now I just say, "Ok, I did that, now what?" while making myself a sandwich.

I tried it the other way, mentioning I was in charge of Tech Support for the American Heart Association for 11 regions of New York, that I'd been in IT for 28 years, that I'd already tried all the normal troubleshooting steps, that I'd like to go directly to Level 2/3 Tech Support, but it's easier to just go with the flow

And at the end, you have a nice sandwich.

20. Get Some Checkboxes

I'm ridiculously competitive. Check boxes are a way of keeping score. At least it starts out that way. Then you start looking at strange experiences as a way of seeing that you're living life, not just existing in it. Let me see if I can give you an example...

I think it all started when I was a little kid. My family had gone to one of those local fairs that show up every six months or so. I was given a couple bucks and allowed to wander freely (this was before we thought child abductors lurked behind every other tree). I had a splendid time, saw all sorts of fun things, got some cotton candy, ate a hotdog, etc. At the end of the day we all met back up. When we got in the car, my mom asked how I'd enjoyed the day. I babbled on about the cool stuff I'd seen and at the end she asked, "What did you think of the little ponies?" Well fuck me. I hadn't seen any ponies. She brought up a few other things I hadn't seen that were epic and I was in tears. I was really little, maybe 6 or 7 years old and I begged to go back so I could see the ponies. But it was too late. We were already driving down the road and the ponies had already been put away. I was heartbroken. So at that age, I vowed I'd never again miss the ponies. That attitude has driven my life. I may not always do the right thing, hell, I'm not even sure I *ever* do the right thing, but it seems to work out and I have a lot of adventures.

So back to the idea of check boxes... I'd say they are great, but you shouldn't get overwhelmed by them. Think of it like what it would be like to bang twins. Would it be cool? I imagine so. Would it be fun? Hell yeah. Would it be something to brag to your buddies about? Unquestionably.

But would you sacrifice your education or your family for it? It depends on how hot they are. No, I'm joking, of course you wouldn't. But setting up a long list of checkboxes takes away the worry that you're missing out.

Everyone has a different set so when you see theirs, you'll learn about things you never considered doing. Because you compare with your buddies, you compare with your family, you compare with your co-workers, in the end, you don't miss out on the ponies.

21. SMILE

You know what simple thing changes the entire world's perception of you?

Smile. That's it. Smile. When you see someone, let a giant broad grin come over your face and I promise people will treat you differently. "Girls don't like me. Boo hoo..." Fuck you. Smile big and let them know you're happy they showed up. Not like a cringing dog, but like a man. Show up at work? Smile. Your boss is so sick and tired of another crop of whiny, bitchy, self-involved and entitled children that you give him/her a big smile and enthusiastically do your job and all of a sudden, glory be, you're the MAN.

But no, it's much easier to bitch and complain. I have a manager at one of my stores who is the living embodiment of this. The cheery bastard never has any problems. He's just happy, upbeat, busts his ass and gets shit done.

You want to change your life? Take 1 week, 1 simple week and smile the whole way through.

22. Learn to Grill a Steak

Every guy should know how to grill a great steak.

1. Buy tenderloins at Sam's Club on Monday (that's the day the new meat comes in at our store).
2. Rub with olive oil.
3. Liberally coat with Omaha steak seasoning.
4. Turn on grill and heat to about 600 degrees.
5. Throw steaks on, 1.5 minutes per side, in the flame.
6. Move them to a non-flame side and cook for 4 minutes per side.
7. Bring them in, let them sit, and enjoy awesome juicy steak goodness.

I was recently shown a trick know when a steak is done. You poke your fingers one at a time into the pad of flesh below your thumb on the same hand – don't tense up your thumb. The firmness will roughly match the firmness of the steak if you bounce the spatula on it.

Pointer finger = rare
Middle finger = medium rare
Ring finger = medium
Pinky finger = well done

Don't forget to allow for 'resting'. After you take them off the grill they will continue to cook.

23. IF YOU REALLY WANT A JOB…

1. Dress in business casual. No tie.
2. Bring a resume.
3. Be positive.
4. Smile the whole time, but not the creepy, "I'm going to eat you" smile.
5. Be assertive.
6. Remember the names of the people they introduce you to.
7. Have fun.

Here's a quick story. I was hiring someone to manage one of my stores. I had over 200 applicants so I brought in the best 12 for a working interview. They worked, I watched them, and when I knew they weren't right I sent them packing. It was down to two, and I really liked this one guy, but the other guy wouldn't leave. He showed up 8:00am, worked the whole day, said he wouldn't accept pay, and left that night at 8:00pm.

He did this for a week. No pay. Just worked to show me he could do the job. As I said, I liked the other guy better, but damn, how could I possibly NOT hire this guy? So I did. Just saying, persistence and enthusiasm can be more important than skillset.

24. TALK TO EVERYONE

You never know who is going to give you really cool advice. My family and I took off on a tour around the country, no special destinations in mind and ended up in Chicago. We were having breakfast and I started bullshitting with a guy at the next table. He thought our trip was cool and recommended we head to Wisconsin Dells. I'd never heard of it. Turns out it's a WHOLE TOWN OF WATERPARKS. It's insane and we spent 3 days there.

You can't overestimate the value of just talking to everyone.

25. THERE ARE GOOD TIMES TO LIE

It has to do with the depth of the lie. "Am I pretty?" is always followed by "Hell yeah! You're beautiful!" Doesn't matter if she's had a bad hair day and she looks like death. You lie your ass off.

If, however, you believe that the long-term benefits favor being straight, then tell the truth, but do it kindly. "I think those clothes don't flatter you. Clothes are supposed to add, not detract from your appearance" is a nice way of saying "You look like ass."

So it's all in the delivery.

26. I'M BORED, WHAT CAN I DO TO PASS THE TIME?

1. Compile a list of people named "Vance" and send them anonymous hate mail.
2. Put on a coat and tie, pretend you're a doorman and spend the day opening doors for people.
3. Find a homeless shelter and volunteer.
4. Make a list of the things you want most in life. Take the top 3 and further enumerate what you'd need to do to make them a reality. Keep doing that for each task until you have a concrete list of things you can do. Then do them.
5. See if there are kids you can help /mentor.
6. See how many times you can rub one out in a day.
7. Go to a park. Rent people puppies.

8. Download a list of the top 100 books and read one of them each day.

9. Go find a lonely girl, tell her, "Hello. I'm trying to experience one day with another person with absolutely no context. I don't want to exchange names, I don't want to tell life stories, I just want to see how we react together with nothing other than what's in front of our eyes." Spend the day with her.

10. Go online and plan your perfect vacation.

This should keep you busy for a bit.

27. You Don't Get To Be Friends With Him!

Warlizard - There is a guy at work that I like a lot as a friend, but not as a boyfriend. I want to make it clear that I like him, but just not that way – how can I do it?

Women and men can't be best friends without having sex. This is a movie concept, not a real-life concept.

Let me break it down for you. He likes you. He wants to have sex with you. He wants to wake up with you in the morning and feed you strawberries.

You don't.

Guys don't work like this. We're programmed to follow through, and the end goal is not to chat about your day or your new boyfriend. If you're interesting enough to be friends with, you're interesting enough to date.

You'll get plenty of advice about how to cool him down, but don't buy it. The idea that you can just talk about other guys and he'll get the hint is crap. He will know that you don't want him, but he'll also stick around because he's hoping that will change. And it won't. You're not going to slowly grow into a deep and abiding love for him. "Someday" is crap. So you have this really cool and interesting guy that you're all excited to be friends with, but yeah, you don't want to date him.

Let me guess - you're not attracted to him, right? Because if you were, you wouldn't even ask.

So you have an ugly/fat guy with a great personality and you're heading down the road toward keeping him in a constant state of frustration and pain just because you want a new friend.

Oh, and you work with him, which makes it 10000 times worse.

You want to know when you get to be friends with this really cool guy you don't want to fuck? When he doesn't want to fuck you. At which point, you will want to fuck him.

28. Are People Who Like Guns Crazy?

A friend of mine who served with me in Desert Storm used to be a fully-pinko ultra-liberal, anti-gun, nutcase who thought that killing bugs was murder. Whenever guns were brought up, she'd rail at length on the statistics, how guns are vastly more likely to kill someone in the home than to be used for protection, how the very concept was outdated, and that we needed to amend the Constitution so that kids could grow up in a world with no war.

This was her favorite topic until one day, when she was at home, and someone tried to break in. Her doors were locked but he started beating in her windows with a crowbar while she sat in terror, holding the phone and waiting for the cops to arrive. It took about 20 minutes and she told me they were the most terrifying moments of her life. She ended up fighting this guy to keep him out, smacking at him with a pan, not knowing where he would try to climb in next, and did so until the cops arrived. They came up sirens a-blazing but the guy left before they could catch him. She got the fuck out, stayed at a friend's house, and the next day she bought a .357 magnum revolver. She trained with it, became proficient, and told me that no matter what, she would never allow herself to be a victim again.

People ask me why I carry a gun. They want to know if I think I'm going to be attacked, or if I'm paranoid, suffering from PTSD. I tell them very simply, the most important people in the world to me are my family. If I were unable to protect them because some crazy fuck decided he wanted to shoot up a place, or go nuts with a machete, I wouldn't be able to live with myself. I train, I'm a very good shot, and I already know that if someone is stupid enough to point a gun at my family, it's the last thing they'll ever do.

29. Career Path

Warlizard - I only have $5000 left, please help me figure out how to get a job that's also a career.

I think it's awesome that you're considering this and it's completely possible. Here's what to do:

Survey the companies in your area and choose 20 you'd like to work for.

Narrow the field down to 5. Be realistic. You're not going to work for Microsoft or Google right out of the gate. The company needs to have fewer than 100 people working at it. It should be close to your house and have a good reputation. Ideally, they should manufacture or write some product that feeds another larger company. It needs to be a privately held company.

Find out who the owners are. Research them. You need to discover what they like. It sounds hard, but really isn't. You can talk to their secretary, hang out at lunchtime restaurants near the business, etc. Figure out what they like. What you're trying to find out is if they are highly educated, in which case stop trying and look elsewhere, or if they are self-made and worked their way up. This is the jackpot. You want to ensure that they won't hold your lack of degrees against you.

You should have a few people in mind by now. The next step is to get in front of them and give them your elevator pitch. There are a few ways to do this, so be creative. One way is to frequent places they go and "bump" into them, but that can easily backfire. You are going to want to make an impression on them and you want it to be a good one, so here's where your money comes in.

By now you've found out who the personal assistant is. If they don't have one, it's the office manager. Doesn't matter. You send flowers to this person and say you're going to call tomorrow to speak with them at 9:00 am sharp.

You send the flowers on Monday so your target is Tuesday at 9:00 am. There is a reason for this. Monday, he/she is going to be slammed. In addition, no one likes Monday. So flowers early in the morning on a Monday will brighten anyone's day, whether girl or guy, plus, he/she is going to be wondering, WTF? Who is this person? You're creating interest.

Prior to this, you should have purchased a nice suit and had it well-tailored. A shitty suit cut to fit you is better than a good suit that hangs, so take your time and get it right. You goddam well better look good.

Tuesday morning you show up, 9:00 am, nice suit, good haircut (get it cut prior to sending the flowers, in case there is a disaster and you need to get it fixed) and this is your opportunity, so don't fuck it up. Prior to this, you should have done a few dry runs at other companies you don't care about, so you feel comfortable. Anyway, you meet with this person and you say this:

"Good morning. My name is XXXXX and I'm interested in 2 minutes and 20 seconds of [Owners Name]'s time. In those 140 seconds, my goal is to convince him/her that I am motivated to work for him/her and to prove it, I will work the first month for one penny. Is there a time on Wednesday when I can get on his/her schedule?"

Now the Executive Assistant is thinking, "WTF? Who the hell is this kid? Are they insane? Crazy?" They may ask for a resume, but DO NOT GIVE them one. The only thing you're doing is asking for 2 minutes and 20 seconds. This pitch is bizarre, especially coming from someone so young, and it will be nearly impossible to resist. One of three things can happen.

- They will set the appointment.
- They will tell you to leave.
- They will tell you that you can see the owner now.

In every case, you're going to see the owner eventually, because dammit, who the hell is this fucking crazy kid? As long as you've done your research and the owner is someone who busted ass to get where he/she is, you'll be in. They won't be able to resist.

When you DO get your 140 seconds, you give your pitch. If you want help tailoring it I will be glad to help you.

30. What is Happiness?

That's a bit complicated to answer and it's going to take a bit of background, but if you're interested enough to ask, I'll certainly oblige.

I hate losing. I hate it more than anything. When I used to shoot pool against girls in bars, they would giggle at me, say that it was just a game and ask why I took it so seriously? I guess because I wanted to be the best, goddamit. I wasn't going to let them win just because they shook their tits at me or rubbed my balls. Yes, I had one girl do that to distract me and no, we didn't know each other. But there's more to it than that and it's a bit complicated. Perhaps we should deconstruct my youth.

I was raised in the church with my Dad as the pastor. It's rough having everyone expect you to be a certain way. A pastor's son is under constant scrutiny – every single thing I did was instantly reported back to my parents and they were judged by my actions. Since they didn't want to look like bad parents who had a rebellious son, discipline was tight. I didn't have the freedom to drink, to smoke, to swear, or to do anything that would reflect poorly on the church without people questioning the validity of my parents' beliefs.

Moving from one church to another every few years didn't help. As soon as things started working out, it was time to leave. So I really had no solid ground to stand on, no friends that lasted more than a year, and I got in a shitload of fights. I guess I was one giant raw nerve by the time I got to a new school and I probably expected the worst out of everyone. This sucked, so after 20 years of living the way someone else wanted me to, I joined the Army.

That didn't fix my problem, but at least no one was running back to my parents every time I had a drink. Still, it did give me the chance to fuck off in new and different ways, just using someone else's rules to live by. I was moderately successful and started to establish myself as a person, not as an appendage to my parents, but there was a fork in the road when I was 27 that changed everything for me.

I had one semester to go to get my degree. I had 7 years of college up until this time, some from the Army, some from before, etc, and I was finally going to get my degree. Well, it was about that time I hooked up with a girl whose sister had a friend who had a friend who offered me a job at one of the top 6 consulting firms in the world. Well damn. I was so close, but what was I going to do with my degree? I mean, not that German isn't a wonderful degree, but damn, how does that translate into anything? So I dropped out of college, took the job, and have been charging since then.

THE WARLIZARD CHRONICLES

See, here's the deal... You're supposed to be a good little drone and get the education (which is indentured servitude after all the loans are factored in), get the job, pay your dues, bust your ass, incrementally climb up the ladder, then retire to spend your golden years in an RV with your aging spouse traveling the country.

Fuck that. I chased money for a long time, now I chase freedom.

31. Dirty Talk

Warlizard - I need some advice. How can I get my man to talk dirty to me?

Well, you need to set the stage for this first.

First, wear something different. I'm not saying you need to wear swastikas and carry a riding crop, but go with something leather, something that shows him he's in for something different. Maybe it's a corset, laced up tight so your breasts heave out the top, or long fishnet stockings, high heeled boots, hot red lipstick, way too much eye shadow... You get the idea.

Instead of flower petals or candles, put on some AC/DC or Dokken. Put a red bulb in the lamp. Tease your hair. You're not looking for romance, you're looking to get fucked hard. Oh yeah, you sure are. He just picked you up at a fucking concert, easy, like the slut you are. All he did was buy you a shot of Jaeger and you were all over him. The drummer had already left and he's the only one who even looked at you, but you need it, you need it bad, and he's the closest one to you.

Your man comes in wanting to know what the hell is going on and where the hell you got a Dokken CD when you just fucking grab his cock. Sluts don't wait for approval, sluts don't need respect, they just need to get fucked. You suck his cock like it's full of Jaeger, you lick his ass, you grab his hand and put it on your wet snatch, you show him that you're a fucking tool, just there to be used.

Sure, he'll be surprised initially, but soon your horny fucking pussy will be sopping wet and he'll be fucking you hard, saying things he never said before, pounding you like you're a piece of meat, and you can have that full body orgasm that only a slut like you can ever dream of.

Failing that, you could just tell him you like dirty talk and politely suggest he comply. Your call. I'd still get that Dokken CD, just in case.

BACK TO THE STORIES

32. BACK IN THE SADDLE

After a breakup, I always feel like shit. It doesn't matter who initiates it – the fact that I'm alone and the intimacy I had is gone is a blow to my confidence. Fortunately, there's a surefire way to fix it. I'm not the first to observe it and I won't be the last, but the best cure for a woman is another woman.

Betty and I had just separated and although it was definitely for the best, I was moping around, avoiding my friends, missing the sex and the house was quiet. I knew what I needed. I needed someone new, someone different, someone who didn't know me or my flaws and who was as seamlessly perfect as only a new girl can be.

At the time I was working at a little computer store and one of my duties was purchasing. I was responsible for keeping the store stocked up with things to sell and this put me in contact with distributors all over the city. One day not too long after the breakup I was talking to one of the reps of a local company and realized she was hitting on me. Well, that was just what I needed so I started flirting back and next thing I knew I had a lunch date for that Saturday. I cleaned up a bit, made sure my clothes passed the sniff test and headed out.

To say I was disappointed would be an epic understatement. She was one of the most physically unattractive people I'd ever seen. She was ugly, bad complected, and going bald. Her greasy thinning blond hair hung limply, her clothes were rumpled and unflattering and she was shaped like a triangle. No chest, big ass. She did, however, have a giant smile and seemed genuinely happy to be there and looking forward to our date.

As you may have picked up by now, my philosophy is to try everything, to go through every door, to live a life of openness and adventure but damn, this one was going to be tough. She was extremely flirty and coming on hard and I knew where this was going. In my mind, the mental struggle ensued. I knew we'd get back and have sex. No question about it. But was it worth it? I decided it was.

There was no way I could do her sober, so we headed back to my place, I poured myself a generous slug of Jim Beam and started pounding it. I was committed to getting back in the saddle, so to speak, and the more I drank, the more fun I started having and you know what? She wasn't really that bad after all! Sure, she didn't have the body type I really liked but hey, she had a body and why shouldn't we have fun? And who was I to discard her just because of her non-traditional looks? She was a human being, dammit. Half-wrecked and full of optimism, I led her back to my bedroom.

Even through the alcoholic haze and impaired judgment, I almost punted when I saw her naked. She wasn't one of those girls who has an awesome body and clothes hide it. It was the other way around and her clothes were bad to start. I remember staring at her in horror and wondering if there were any ways out for me. Her tits were like tube socks, and one was longer than the other. She had zits on her chest. She had bad teeth. She was wholly unappealing, but dammit, I needed to get back in the saddle and she was there.

I closed my eyes and tried to concentrate on some of my more interesting conquests but this chick was crazy annoying and wouldn't shut up. Every word she said took me out of fantasy-land and reminded me of the person beneath me. The alcohol filter started to wear off and my good feelings went with it. I started being a real jerk. Every time she was about to orgasm, I'd stop, just to be annoying, but that turned her on even more and she thought I was teasing her to be sexy. Dear god, how was I going to get her out? While I was pondering my exit strategy, she said, "I wonder what it would be like in the other place. I wonder if it would hurt?"

Oh for fuck's sake.

I had just ended a relationship with a girl who needed her ass plunged daily and the VERY NEXT GIRL is trying to coquettishly lead me down the same highway? Not just no, but HELL no. Oh, and, by the way, you know that little brown ring, the reason girls get ass-bleaching? Well she had one too. But it was damn near the size of a coaster. No way in hell I was doing that.

Anyway, she was beneath me, arms above her head, tube sock drooping into each armpit, and my phone rang. Hey, any excuse to stop, right? I got up to answer it and it was my Dad.

He was just calling to say Hi, and the Beast decided it would be funny to mess with me, so she started blowing me while I was still on the phone. Ok, now I had two choices:

1. Get off the phone.
2. Get off while ON the phone.

I chose the latter, just to be able to say I'd done it. I closed my eyes, let her finish me off, hung up with my Dad, and told her we'd get together soon. She told me next time we'd have a threesome with her pregnant, bisexual roommate.

Dear god.

There was just no way so I avoided her until she stopped calling. I'm not proud of my reaction but hey, at least I was back in the saddle.

33. CELEBRITY SIGHTING

A guy who owed me a few grand was ducking me. I had paid him cash for some LCD monitors and he didn't deliver them. After a few weeks of him not calling me, I got pissed and drove out to L.A. I walked into his warehouse and stood quietly behind him with my arms crossed until he turned around and noticed me.

I've never seen anyone so scared in my life. I have been told I can be intimidating and I thought he was going to have a heart attack when he saw me silently watching him. We had a conversation and he decided that since I'd had to drive all the way out to L.A. he'd put me up for the night.

Well, this was near Hollywood and one of my favorite hotels in the world is there, a really cool place called The Renaissance. It's right next to the Kodak Theater and by the walk of fame. I concluded my business with the bastard and drove over to my hotel. I pulled up, tossed the valet my keys and was about to walk inside when I noticed this guy by the front door. He was obviously some sort of director or producer, because he was wearing really ostentatious glasses and a silk scarf in 90 degree weather.

Next to him was someone I recognized. Holy shit, it was Clive Owen! If you ever wondered how someone could be a movie star and why they'd make it over someone else, well, let me tell you, this guy was impressive. I swear, just standing there, he looked cool as hell. Nice suit, no tie, open collar, looking off into the distance. I have never been that cool in my life, but I like to mess with people, so I walked up and said, "Holy cow! Can I get a picture with you?"

I made sure I was looking roughly between them and was wearing sun glasses so my eyes weren't visible. He said, "Sure." I pulled out my iPhone, set it to the camera, handed it to him and said, "You know how to work it?"

He looked like a safe had dropped on him. I moved over, put my arm around the director (or whoever he was) and smiled. Poor Clive. Completely shocked, he held up the camera and took a picture. I took my phone back, said thanks, and walked inside. I heard the director guy laughing so hard I thought he was going to throw up.

Hey, everyone can use a bit of humility, right?

34. PARKER

Parker was the guy I always wanted to be. He had movie-star looks, was charismatic as hell, and life always just seemed to go his way. He was a former golden gloves boxer and just flat-out cool as shit. One hooker told him that he was the man she'd waited for all her life and she'd leave right that minute if he'd take her with him.

He was in Military Intelligence as well, but when we deployed to the Gulf, he decided he wanted to have more fun so he transferred to the infantry company in our Battalion. I know that doesn't sound like much, but you can't just change groups in a war. He wasn't trained; he just thought it would be fun. I once saw him knock out one of his teeth with a hammer and a screwdriver because it was bothering him. Other people would have been bothered by that, but not ol' Parker.

The other thing was he'd fuck anyone. He just didn't care. Beautiful, ugly, it just didn't matter. I remember one time he showed up at my apartment at about 2am (sounds bad, but I'd just walked in. The bars closed in

Frankfurt at 2). He had some giant beast with him. He wanted some place to fuck and figured I'd hook him up. Hell, of course I would.

Anyway, we decide to head up to Holland one weekend to have fun and do some acid. I can't remember everyone who was there, but I know a couple Delta Company (the infantry company in our battalion) guys, Parker, and I for sure.

Anyway, they had some friends in a town called Eindhoven where we could crash, so that was our destination. We got there and Parker had an extra few tabs of acid, so he hooked me up and we all dropped.

After about 30 minutes, things got a bit strange. I decided I needed to be alone, so I went upstairs into the bedroom and lay down on the bed, listening to Pink Floyd.

The windows had those vertical blinds, slats really, and the shadows cast looked like bars on a jail cell. At least they did for me. So I sat there bugging for a while, then someone came up and talked to me for a while. Not sure who it was, but probably someone who just wanted to make sure I was ok. I was, but you ever had an itch that you just HAD to scratch?

Well, I had one in the center of my chest. So I kept scratching it. And it was kinda hot, so I was sweating a bit. Or maybe it was blood. It was dark in the room and I kept scratching, thinking I might be digging a hole into my skin, but couldn't stop, and was on the verge of a giant meltdown when ol' Parker turned on the light and came in. I was pretty much fine after that, and spent the next few hours just sitting there chilling out, enjoying the sensations.

After a while I walked downstairs, and started doing that pope thing where you do the sign of the cross on people who are in front of you. I think it's called genuflecting or something like that. Anyway, I was stumbling around anointing everyone and someone asked me how I was doing. I told them I was doing great, that I knew EVERYTHING now.

They told me they knew where I was coming from, that they knew EVERYTHING too. I told them they were all fools and knew nothing, that I *really* knew everything, but they were smoking hash and were really mellow, so it all worked out.

The next day we all went out to the clubs and the most amazingly gorgeous women I'd ever seen were hanging out, each more beautiful than the next. The cool part was they didn't get much of a chance to speak English, so they were lining up at the bar to buy us drinks.

We were all pretty wrecked when I spotted the most insanely hot girl I'd ever seen. She would have ruled any runway she walked down with ease. She had flawless skin, perfect dark, straight hair, red lipstick, a tight black dress that clung to every perfect curve of her body and I vowed to make her mine.

I went up to her and did my best to lay down my game, but it didn't go well. Maybe it was that I wanted her too much, maybe it was how drunk I was, but she smiled kindly at me and looked the other way. Parker walked up to her and said, "You have funny hair." and they left. That was it. He was just like that. He ended up working for the CIA, then running a couple strip clubs.

BACK TO THE STORIES

I never met anyone else in my life who lived so far outside of the place the rest of us did. It was just as if the rules didn't apply to him. The best looking girl in our battalion (that's not saying much) was a blond girl named Theresa. Ol' Parker fucked her, then went up to her boyfriend and said, "I just fucked your girlfriend. What are you going to do about it?" Now her boyfriend was a total dick (he's a cop in Florida now) so we all thought that was funny as hell. Dickhead knew he'd get killed if he started anything so he didn't. He just walked away in shame and I stood there with a giant grin on my face.

I think one of the major differences between me and Parker is he never knew his limits. I've always backed off when I realized something wasn't working. Parker has been a millionaire several times and now he's sleeping on someone's couch, completely broke.

The lesson here is to try everything, but do it with your eyes open.

35. Breaking Up Using Porn

Never stick your dick in crazy. We all know the concept, but what if you don't know when you meet her that she's batshit nuts? This is the story of one such girl and how I managed to finally get rid of her.

Back when I was at the Defense Language Institute in Monterey, CA, life was good. I had great friends, money, freedom, or at least as much freedom as anyone in the Army could have. Weekdays were spent learning German and weekends were spent getting wrecked and having uninhibited sex with an ever-revolving group of military women.

One day, my buddy Krup, his girlfriend and I were going down into Monterey to see a movie. A hot girl in bicycle shorts was walking up the hill as we were walking down and she smiled at me, more by reflex than anything else. Well, I don't need much of an opening, so I said, "Heya. I'm Warlizard, we're going down to see a movie and could use a fourth. Wanna come?"

I didn't expect her to say yes, but Raquel surprised me by agreeing so we ended up spending the rest of the day together, getting along famously. She said she had a boyfriend at Ft. Ord, an Army base a few miles away, but that never stopped me, so I kept making plans to meet her for lunch, breakfast, etc. Once she was good and hooked, I cut off contact and said that I really didn't see any point in hanging with a girl who had a boyfriend. The next day, I came back and there was a teddy-bear sitting in front of my door with a note to expect her that night, boyfriend-free. SWEET! I love winning.

A little bit about Raquel. She was brunette and slender, big smile and had a smoking bod. The only thing I didn't like about her was her hair. She was rocking the "wet look" and it didn't work for her. Being a flaming dick, I pointed out that I wasn't a big fan of that look and she said she was sorry, that she'd change it. Huh? Really? I didn't expect that, I was mostly just running my mouth.

Anyway, the big night came and she showed up at my room, looking hot (except for the hair) and ready to be mine! We started to get physical, starting slowly, making out, until we were almost naked. All she had on were her panties and she wouldn't take them off. I told her my standard bullshit line about spending 30 minutes down below and she said that she couldn't, that it was a bad time of the month. Ah. Good point. But dammit, I was horny and didn't feel like doing the 2 mile run the next morning with blue balls, so I asked what she was up for.

She said she didn't want to leave me in pain and could give me a great handjob. Quickly I realized that her definition of "great" and mine were separated by a gulf of chafed genitals and misplaced enthusiasm. I knew I had to do something quickly, before all the skin was gone, so I told her to wait and that I'd be right back.

I threw on some clothes and started banging on doors, trying to find someone who had something, anything I could use to place some sort of barrier between my delicate junk and her calloused hands. The only person in his room was my buddy Gabe. Quick word about Gabe. He was ultra conservative, not so much about religion, but about everything else. As an example, he bought a Volvo because of its safety rating. Everyone else was buying Cameros, Trans-Ams, Corvettes, etc, but he bought a Volvo. Great guy though.

Anyway, he looked at me like I was nuts when I asked him for some sort of lube but all he had was strawberry scented tanning oil. That was fine with me, so I grabbed the sandy bottle and headed back to my room. It worked as hoped, I made my run the next morning, and what did I care? I got the girl. So I had to wait… Whatever. Granted, my room smelled like strawberries for weeks, but it was worth it.

The next day I came home a bit late from school. I'd stopped off at the dayroom to shoot a few games of pool and when I got back to my room, I was stunned to find her there, ironing my uniforms. My roommate gave me a look and asked if he could talk to me outside. It turned out that she'd shown up right after school ended, got my clothes, washed them, then came up and started ironing them. He suggested that I marry this girl before she woke up or found out what a horrible person I was.

He also suggested I was a complete rat-bastard who didn't deserve this. He was right.

Raquel said that she just wanted to help out and why shouldn't she do my laundry with hers? I couldn't think of a single reason. Not one. She started spending more and more time in my room and one day, her hair didn't look wet anymore.

I told her she looked awesome and asked why she she'd changed it. She looked like she was about to cry and said she'd gotten lice from a roommate and had to put some special stuff in her hair. Um, ok. I reassured her that these things happened and it didn't make any difference to me.

At this point, I would have agreed to about anything because I was tired of not fucking. I'd put in the time, dammit, so how about let's get this party started, ok? Of course, I didn't say this. I was understanding and patient, so a few days later when she said she was ready, so I was I.

In all fairness to her, my clothes never looked better, so I didn't feel that badly about not having sex, but I was definitely ready. So was she, so we went at it like crazy. She was enthusiastic, easily orgasmic, and her body was spectacular. All-in-all, she was fantastic. She was in my room most of the time, slept there every night, and my roommate hated me. He seemed to think it was unfair that I, a well-known asshole would have a hot girl at my beck and call, who did my laundry, cleaned the room, and fucked the hell out of me. I didn't know she was crazy though. She seemed so normal.

I had a party a couple nights later and had some friends over, including a couple girls I'd slept with.

With them it had been casual, more like a backrub than anything else, but because we were so relaxed, we were a bit more affectionate than was appropriate. Certainly more than Raquel was comfortable with.

We all had a few drinks and were relaxing, watching TV, when out of the blue, Raquel grabbed my balls, looked one of the girls dead in the eyes and said, with no hint of humor, "See this? This is mine. Whenever I want. All mine." My friend froze and finally managed to say, "Um, ok, that's yours." Raquel nodded, released me, and went back to watching the movie. My friend shot me a wide-eyed look of "What the hell, Dude?" I had nothing to say, and if I'm being candid, I thought it was kinda cool. I liked a girl that wasn't a doormat.

Not too long after that, I asked her why we waited so long to have sex and she said that she had crabs and wanted to make sure they were gone. Oh Jesus. Crabs. Nice. Apparently she'd gotten them from her former boyfriend and didn't want me to catch them. Mighty considerate, I thought. What a great girl. What a great, possessive, batshit-crazy girl.

Things went downhill fast. One day she was peaches and cream, the next she was telling me that she really didn't want me hanging around those other girls, that they were trying to steal me away from her. Huh? I didn't point out we'd already had sex and they were just buddies, albeit sexy buddies who liked to fuck.

I let things go but I started to see her everywhere. If I had lunch, she was there to eat with me. At night, she was there as soon as I got to my room. I never would have put up with it, but my room was so clean and my laundry was so well-starched and ironed. Plus, as earlier noted, she was a demon in bed.

Finally, I decided I wasn't going to deal with her paranoid craziness anymore and told her that I thought we should cool it, that she was awesome, but I felt things had gotten too high pressure. She told me that I was wrong, that everything was fine, but that she'd give me a little space if that was what I needed. Turned out, her definition of space and mine weren't the same. Actually, nothing changed at all. My room was surgically clean, my clothes were perfect and she wouldn't leave. Something had to be done.

My room was unusual in that I had a TV and a VCR. There was a TV in the dayroom but I was the only person in the building who had one in his bedroom. Because of this, I had a constant group of people wanting to watch movies with me, and by accident, Wednesday night turned into Porn Night. The entire hall would crowd into my room and we'd watch whatever was brought.

Sometimes it was classic porn night, with "Deep Throat", "Behind the Green Door", and other seminal works. Other times we'd go with something new. Remember, this was long before the internet and if people wanted to watch porn, there were only two options – magazines and video tapes.

Anyway, Wednesday was a popular night and everyone looked forward to it. So when Raquel said that she wanted to talk, I told her that it was Wednesday and I was busy. There was no way I was going to cancel Porn Night.

8:00pm came and the room filled up. Rachel had been there since about 5 and I just refused to talk to her. I had buddies there and I wasn't up for a big discussion. She kept trying and I kept deflecting. Finally, when the first porno kicked off, she stood up, screamed at me that I was a giant fucking asshole and left. Everyone clapped.

See, my roommate had been telling them about her for a while and everyone knew she was nuts. Still, she sure was fun. My clothes returned to their former rumpled state, my room was only cleaned for inspections, and life went back to normal. She disappeared and I forgot about her.

A few months later I graduated and was shipped off to my new duty station where we were to learn the mechanics of Military Intelligence. I hated it. The new base was in Texas and it was ridiculously hot there. Still, everyone I'd known at DLI was there, so getting to a new base was just a change of location, not of tone. A few weeks after I'd arrived, I was chilling in my room with a few buddies and having a few drinks when there was a knock at the door. I opened it up and there stood Raquel, in a flimsy negligee, holding a pizza box. "Um, hi Raquel, what's up?"

"I heard you were here and had some extra pizza."

"Yeah, thanks, that's cool." I took the pizza box and she turned and walked away. Now here's the awkward part. I was on the first floor in a room that faced out to the quad. So Rachel had walked all the way across the quad wearing next to nothing to bring me pizza. I closed the door, opened up the pizza box and sure enough, there was a hot pizza inside. Score! I looked up and both my buddies were staring at me with their mouths wide open.

"Um, Dude? Who the hell is that?"

"Oh yeah. That's Raquel. We used to hang."

"Are you a complete moron? Go get her."

I have a bad memory and I thought back to how much fun we had, completely discounting the crazy, decided I could use a refresher, and ran after her. I caught up with her right as she reached her room and started to go into my routine, when she burst out crying.

Ok, I'm SO not about tears. I stood there awkwardly and she threw her arms around me, sobbing. I asked her what was wrong and when she could finally stop long enough to speak, she said, "War, Jesus loves you and wants you to come into his fold. All you have to do is ask."

What. The. Fuck.

I have to admit, of all the things I could have imagined her saying, that was never on the list. In all the times we'd been together, she'd never mentioned Jesus, religion, church, or Christianity. I was stunned. "Um, what?"

"He loves you War. You're empty inside and you need him to bring you into his fullness of grace." I stood there for a second, then finally blurted out, "Look Rachel, thanks for the pizza, I need to run."

And I bolted. Cowardly? Yeah, probably, but what would you do? I saw her every once in a while until she graduated, but never spoke to her again. I'm sure she's somewhere cleaning house, doing laundry, fucking the hell out of her man, and going to church. Good for her.

36. The Irish Girl

I was pretty bad when I was younger. I was in Germany... shit, so many of the best stories start that way. Anyway, I had kind of a bad reputation with the Irish girls. I had been with this one who was a bit chunky for my taste, but was cool as hell. I was finally going to nail her after trying for almost a month, so expectations were high. I was going down on her when she said, "But War, I want a relationship!"

Well fuck. I didn't. She was cool, but not cool enough to keep as a girlfriend. So I stopped mid-lap and said maybe it was better that we just stayed friends. That was one of the few times in my life I didn't fuck someone I could have. All I had to say was, "I do TOO!" and it would have been ON!

Anyway, a week or so later I was at the Irish pub in Frankfurt and she was there with one of her friends, some chick named Breedah. At least that's how it was pronounced. It had some strange-ass spelling and I just don't remember it.

Breedah was being really strange to me, and I couldn't figure it out. We all had a bunch of drinks and finally she blurted out that I was a bastard and she knew all about me, that I was a dog, etc. Whatever. A few more drinks and she starts getting all weepy about how she had a one night stand with this guy and then she was so ashamed that she almost killed herself. Challenge accepted!

We ended up heading back to my place where I promised myself I would make this the greatest night of her young life. I used every trick I'd learned, put her in every position I could, fucked as long as possible and (in one of the proudest moments of my life) as she lay panting in exhaustion from her multiple orgasms, she told me I was Jesus Christ.

I'm not sure if she was hallucinating or just complementing me, but I felt pretty good about it. Anyway, I never saw her again. I guess a night of sex with me didn't make her want to kill herself, so that's something.

A year later, I saw the original girl who'd wanted the relationship at a local bar. By now, she'd lost the weight, figured out how to dress and was smokin' hot. We made out a bit but she said she was with her boyfriend now and I'd missed my shot. Turned out her boyfriend was a good friend of mine (Gabe - the one who lent me the strawberry sun-tan lotion) so I kissed her goodbye and wished her the best.

37. THE TWISTED OSTRICH

Everyone has worked with someone they hated. I've never had a job where there wasn't someone who made my life miserable, or whose very presence pissed me off. Usually you just have to put up with them, but every once in a great while, you can get even...

"Dave" was a dick. Stoop-shouldered, balding, in his 50's, Dave was a patronizing and irritating bastard. He'd been at IBM his whole career, had been making good money, and hated contractors. He thought they were bad for the company, that the only people worth a shit were regular employees, and he made it his personal priority to fuck with all of us. Nothing overt, but constant subtle pressure was put on everyone whose badge said "Contractor" on it. I think he developed this attitude from working with the guys from India, probably because they were so soft-spoken and accommodating, but maybe he was just a racist. I dunno, but whatever the reason, he took every opportunity to send us on little errands, wouldn't get back to us if we needed something, criticized anything we did and generally made our lives hell in a way that couldn't be directly protested.

I was pretty good friends with the guy sharing the room with him, another full-time employee and one day "Robert" called me up. "War. We're going for coffee."

"Um, ok, let me just finish up a few things."

"You don't understand. We need coffee NOW!"

Right. I headed over to his office and he met me about halfway there. His eyes were shining with glee but he wouldn't tell me what was going on until we had our coffee in the cafeteria. Once we finally had a table, he said, "Ok. Dave's a fetish wrestler!"

"Huh?"

"He's a fetish wrestler!"

"Dude, I've got nothing. WTF is a fetish wrestler?"

It turned out that there were men who pay women to wrestle them into submission. Some of them did it as a sort of hobby and others were extremely serious about it. Dave was one of the latter. Several times a year, he'd tell his wife he was meeting up with old Army buddies but went to Fetish Wrestling conventions instead. They were highly organized, had rings set up for use, referees to score the matches and everything. I never quite understood the need for refs, but hey, it's not my fetish. There were web pages devoted to the women who were available to wrestle and Dave's favorite was a woman named "Red Robin". She was a little tiny woman who was an absolute beast and he paid her thousands of dollars every time he'd go to one of these conventions for her to wrestle him for about 20 minutes per match. We went back to my office and pulled up Red Robin's website.

"Why does he pay this woman to wrestle him? She's ugly as hell. Do they fuck after?"

"He says no."

"Let me get this straight... Dave lies to his wife, flies out to California to have an ugly woman named Red Robin wrestle him into submission, pays her $400 per match, and DOESN'T fuck her?"

"Yep."

"Bullshit."

I went on to the main wrestling site and started reading Dave's posts. And there were a ton of them. He talked in great detail and depth about the "sport", had invented his own move, called the "Twisted Ostrich", and told stories about amazing matches he'd won and lost.

Look, I'm all about people's private lives remaining private, and I probably wouldn't have done anything if he hadn't so consistently been a fuck to me. But he had, so game on! I registered a fake account under the name Sue_Plex on the wrestling web site and started corresponding with him.

I started by asking him some technical questions about the Twisted Ostrich, but it wasn't long until he started asking me personal questions. As time went by, I fleshed out the character so within about a month he had become quite good friends with Miss Plex. I told him I was a late-20s single lawyer living in D.C. My marriage had ended because my husband just didn't understand my interest in such a harmless sport. It was so nice to talk to someone like him who really understood me.

BACK TO THE STORIES

It was unbelievably satisfying. Every time he'd send me on some stupid errand, I'd think of how he was confessing his private life to the character I'd created. Oh, and he lied his ass off. He dropped a good ten years and his wife somehow. Finally, he asked for a picture. Well, I'd already downloaded a whole set of a girl who looked about that age, and the photos didn't look professional. I started with a simple one and he gushed about how hot I was. Over the next few weeks, I sent him more and more photos, each more revealing than the last, until the girl was fully nude, but didn't look posed.

He started trying to be really sexy, and started talking about how the best way to end a good wrestling match was with sex. Hold the phones! He'd told Robert that there wasn't any sex at the matches! I probed a bit and he finally admitted he had sex with the girls he wrestled.

I fucking knew it!

They were hookers working a special kind of crowd. It made more sense he was spending 400 bucks per match. I amped up the sexy talk too, including wrestling into it. It was gold.

He was hooked. His work slowed down, he became obsessed with Sue_Plex and quite frankly, my work suffered as well having to answer all his notes. Fortunately, he didn't notice because he was too busy sending off love letters. Now it was driving me nuts, because here was this creepy 50'ish guy who was still giving me a daily ration of shit but was secretly having an online affair with a character I'd created. Robert and I had a ton of fun fucking with the poor guy, but one day, he called me up again – "War. Coffee. Now."

At the cafeteria he told me that Dave had another "Army reunion" coming up and we should see if we could get him to come to D.C. to meet "Sue" instead. Hmmmm. Genius! I sent Dave an email and said we should get together some time. Boom. In a flash, he responded that he had been thinking the same thing and had some time off in a few weeks. Would I be interested in him coming to visit?

Yes. Yes I would.

As Sue, I arranged to meet him in D.C. at local hotel. As the day approached, Dave became more and more excited and fucked with us less and less. He still tried, but the conviction and heat wasn't there anymore. Robert and I were going nuts, having to act like nothing was going on while Dave prattled on about how happy he was to hook up with his old Army buddies, what a fun trip it would be, how he was hoping he didn't get pinned down by the snow, etc. I guess he thought he was being clever, but since we already knew the entire story, it just came across as pathetic.

He left early on a Friday to catch his flight, smiling like a champ.

Tuesday morning, he showed up looking like his best friend had died. We asked what was wrong and he tried to play it off like he was just tired from his long weekend, but as soon as he could, he sent Sue a message asking what the hell had happened and why hadn't she showed up? We waited to respond until after lunch. He was a basket case. Finally we fired back a furious message that we'd called his house on Friday just to leave him a message and some WOMAN ANSWERED! We said we'd pretended to give her a survey and we knew about his wife and 4 kids. So he'd been lying to us all along. Basically, we went batshit crazy on him. We told him if he ever tried to contact us again, we'd tell his wife everything. We waited for him to get the email, watched him surreptitiously read it and then we watched him have a meltdown.

He started sweating like crazy, called his wife to check on her, and finally left early. He was never the same after that. He pretty much stopped messing with contractors and kept to himself. We never sent him any more emails and he never sent any to Sue. My contract ended not too long after that and that was the last I heard of him.

It couldn't have happened to a nicer guy.

38. THE GREATEST LIE I EVER TOLD

I was in Hollywood on business staying at the Renaissance and was in the bar downstairs bullshitting with a couple of club promoters. An insanely hot girl came up, sat there for a bit, and asked what I did. Here was my response:

"I refill bowling balls."
"Huh?"
"Actually, I own a company that refills them. Not regular ones, of course, but the ones that professionals use."

She looked a bit skeptical.

"Ever notice how when the professionals bowl the ball seems to jerk to the left or right really hard right before the pins?"

She nodded.

"That's because there is a liquid core in the middle. Over time, however, it degrades, so we have to extract the ana-viscous fluid, refill the ball, plug the hole we made, make sure it's perfectly balanced, then re-polish it. It takes a few weeks to get it perfect, but it's worth it."

She looked at me dully for a second, then brightened and said, "Wow, that's really cool! I always wondered why the bowling balls did that!"

We talked a bit more and she wandered off to smoke a cig. I waited until she was out of earshot and said to the club guys, "Hey, thanks for backing me up."

They replied, "What do you mean? That's the greatest thing ever! Any time a girl asks me what I do I'm going to tell her that."

I laughed and said, "Yeah, but thanks for not ratting me out."

They looked confused and said, "What do you mean?"

Sigh. I guess I was convincing.

39. I RUN FROM THE COPS

I wasn't always the responsible guy I am now. There was a pretty long stretch where I just didn't care what I did. I've always been an aggressive driver, but back then I was crazy. I was drifting around corners back in the 90s, pulling power slides, and basically endangering myself and everyone around me.

I can't remember how many tickets I was given, but I think it was about 12. My license had been revoked for non-payment, and with no license, you can't have insurance, so my insurance had been cancelled.

This didn't stop me from driving, or even for speeding. The only time I did the speed limit was when I was driving home from the bars. One point I'd like to clarify – I never drove drunk. I learned my lesson from a very close call years before and hadn't done it since. But aside from that, I was a demon on wheels.

I was driving an Isuzu Impulse which I'd bought for cheap and it was a little rocket. I always preferred driving a stick and this car handled like a dream.

BACK TO THE STORIES

It was only a matter of time until all the tickets caught up with me, and I knew it would be expensive when they did. One day, I was driving home, came up over a rise, and blew right past a cop who was driving the opposite direction. I knew I was screwed. I was doing at least 65 in a 45 and he looked straight at me when we passed. I quickly ran through my head what my options were.

1. Pull over to the side of the road and wait. He would see my license was suspended and I didn't have insurance, then I would get a ton of tickets.

2. Keep on going and see if he turned around. Maybe he wasn't going to throw on his lights.

3. Run.

I chose the third option. The first left wasn't that far away so I hit the brakes hard, shifted into 2nd, popped the clutch and drifted around the corner. There were trees everywhere and about 50 yards down the road was a dirt road mostly obscured by branches and overgrowth that went up a hill. In a split second, I decided to go up it.

I exploded up the hill, through the branches, slung the car around and waited. About 30 seconds later, the cop blew by. I tried to pull out, but the car wouldn't move. WTF?

When I'd slung the car around, I'd managed to bounce my rear differential onto a stump. My back wheels weren't even touching the ground. I got out, looked at my stupid wheels that were only about an inch off the dirt, tried to push the car off, but it wasn't happening. Then, through the trees I saw something terrible. The cop was coming back.

Ever have that sinking feeling that tells you that you are irretrievably fucked, and there is simply no point in fighting anymore? No matter what I tried at this point, there was no way out of this situation. I had blown my chance to get away, and for some reason the cop was coming back.

I thought about it for 10 seconds and figured, better just head down and take responsibility. As I emerged from the branches that covered the road, the cop approached my position. I held out my arm and gave him the "I fucked up and you got me" face. He had already begun to slow down, but I was hoping to get some points. Hey, if I could deflect some of the pain, it was worth it.

He stopped, got out of his vehicle and I said, "Bah, you got me."

His first question: "Why did you run?"

"I knew you were going to come after me and I didn't want a ticket."

"Where's your car?"

"Up the hill."

We walked up the hill and there she was, truly stumped.

He looked at me with a combination of awe at my misfortune and barely contained mirth.

"You're stuck?"

"Yep."

"If I bring out dogs, they gonna find any drugs out here? I can have them here in 10 minutes."

"Nope."

"You really ran just because you didn't want a ticket?"

"That's right."

He looked at me sadly.

"I was only going to give you a warning. You were only going 8 over the speed limit."

Huh? I knew I'd been going much faster than that. But if he thought so I wasn't going to try to change his mind.

"Come back with me. Let me see your license."

I stood there by the side of his vehicle while he checked my license. The results came back and I saw his eyebrows rise. He mouthed a silent "Wow."

Then he started to write. I'd say he wrote for a good 15 minutes. I can't remember how many tickets I got, but it was absurd. I think I had about 6 or 7. He handed them to me and said, "You need to get this taken care of."

"I will."

"You know I could take you to jail right now for evading arrest, right?"

"I do."

"You know why I came back?"

"No, and I wasn't going to ask, but I'd really like to know."

"This road is a dead-end."

Fuck.

He took off, left me my license and my car. I still don't know why he didn't have it impounded. I called a tow-truck and had them pull me off the stump, then drove home. With that many tickets, I expected to be car-less and license-less for the foreseeable future. Here's the messed-up part:

I got a lawyer who specialized in tickets. He had some sort of arrangement with the judge, so they made the tickets go away. It cost me a couple grand, plus the fines, but after all was said and done, I had 3 points on my fully-restored license. So for a suspended license, no insurance, speeding multiple times, running from the cops and reckless driving, I got 3 points.

Ain't the justice system grand?

40. Plug in the Strobe Light

My life revolved around women for a long time and most of the trouble I got into had something to do with a girl. In keeping with my philosophy of doing everything, trying everything at least once and never holding back when an opportunity presented itself, I asked out every girl I thought was pretty or interesting. It didn't always end well…

Example: I was at the Defense Language Institute learning German and at that time, we weren't allowed to have women in the room after about 12:00AM. It was an Article 15 offense, so we had to be discreet. Anyway, I loved having loud boisterous parties and would put strobe lights in the window to let people know when the festivities were kicking off.

The reason my parties were so much fun is that there were always women there. In a pretty short time I was known as the guy with the booze, music, TV, etc., so while some guys would try to get the girls alone, I would just crank up the music, pass out the booze and people would show up. Since the rooms were pretty small, it was standing room only so people would come early so they didn't have to fight to get inside.

Some guys would get hung up on one special girl, but that wasn't my style. I was so casual that I would just hook up with the last girl to leave the party. It was a far more effective method than trying all evening to score with a girl only to find out too late she had a fiancée back home. At 12:00AM I'd shut off the music, turn off the strobe and kick everyone out. The girl who stuck around, usually to "use the bathroom real quick" and hid until everyone was gone was the one who wanted to hook up.

Anyway, I remember a girl who stuck around one night who I had no idea would be waking up with me. She had "Wicked Witch of the West" striped stockings which kind of tied into a fantasy of mine and she was a loud, bouncy ride. She was fun and passionate and we had a blast, although we might have annoyed my neighbors.

The next afternoon I was called into the Platoon Sergeant's office and he was pissed. No, he was beyond pissed. He was fired the fuck up. Mad as hell, face red, etc. He also had short man's disease, so he's looking up at me, accusingly and I had no idea why. Finally he comes out with, "You make me sick."

I sat there baffled. I had ZERO idea what he was talking about. He badgered me for about 30 minutes trying to get me to admit something and finally said, "War, fucking a girl doggie-style while she's vomiting into your toilet is just goddam disgusting!"

This was the last thing I could have expected. Oh, I was sure he had heard I'd had a girl stay there overnight or something, but the story was so absurd that it had to be a joke. Since he was such a ramrod-straight type of guy, people liked to mess with him and I think they got him good with this one. Anyway, he had no proof and I kept denying it so he had nothing to do but let me go. He spent the rest of my time there trying to catch me, but as I said, I'm lucky.

As I look back at those crazy times, the thing that hits me is that although people were jealous of the parties I had, the women who liked to hang around and the fun, it was their fault. I was the one who put the strobe in the window and turned it on. I bought the TV and the stereo and created the atmosphere for the party. I didn't do anything that any of them couldn't have done too, but the difference was that I actually did it. I'm not saying that you need to have crazy drunken parties to have fun in life, but if you don't try, you'll be the person in the wings, waiting for something fun to happen and I'll be the guy in the middle having the time of his life.

41. THE OLD ANNOYING GUY

I own a couple computer stores and a few months back, I went to a computer onsite to help out an old guy who couldn't get on the internet. I don't normally do onsites, but there was a scheduling issue, so I figured I'd just knock it out real quick, make a few bucks and keep my employees working in the store.

An old guy in his late 60s answered the door and I started working on his system. He was annoying and distracting as hell, talking at length about his sexual conquests, how he flew to Asia every year and spent a week with prostitutes, how the best shower he had was with a 17 year old Asian prostitute, how perfect her tits were, etc. I just wanted him to keep his exploits to himself and let me finish.

A buddy of mine was in from out of town and since he was with me, he helped by distracting the old bastard, who wouldn't just shut the hell up. On and on he went, spewing the most graphic details about the truly stratospheric number of Asian prostitutes he'd had sex with and it was driving me nuts. Finally something caught my attention. I realized he had just mentioned that he had significant health issues stemming from his time "over there". My buddy asked him what he had done over there, and it turned out he was in the Army and had been captured in Viet Nam, then spent 3 years in a POW camp being tortured.

Wait, what? 3 years? I couldn't help but stop what I was doing and instead of seeing an annoying old guy, I saw a broken man who, some 40 years earlier had done more than I will ever do, had suffered more than I will ever suffer, and had somehow managed to make it through, heavy reliance on Asian prostitutes notwithstanding.

He continued on in equally graphic detail telling us what they had done to him. I wanted to throw up. They fucking broke him. It was horrible. And somehow, he made it through it, although he was unable to have any semblance of a relationship after. His wife left him. His friends left him. He lives alone now, in the twilight of his life and all he has left is the hookers.

Yeah, I didn't charge him. When he asked me why, I told him he already spent 3 years paying and there was no fucking way I was going to charge him again.

I left there feeling like an asshole and wondering how many other people I've snap-judged and maybe if I'd just had a little more information I would have shut my arrogant mouth and felt a little goddam compassion.

42. Getting Even

We were in KKMC (King Khalid Military City, Saudi Arabia) when we heard we were going home. We'd been sitting around for a few months while the powers-that-be considered our fate and we were restless as hell. No one knew if we'd be staying for another 6 months, re-deploying back to Germany, or sent somewhere new, so we were going stir-crazy.

Some General somewhere finally realized that keeping German and Russian linguists sitting around doing nothing was pointless, so he decided our unit was going to be decommissioned and the best place to do that was back at our home base in Germany.

We all had our reasons to be excited. Some missed their kids, some were leaving the Army when we got back, others had pets, but for me, it was simple. I missed partying. I wanted bourbon, I wanted cider, I wanted women, and dear god I wanted the incredible street gyros in Sachsenhausen.

If you read the story of the French girl, you'll remember that she was my girlfriend before we left and

BACK TO THE STORIES

I had never responded to any of her letters. I still don't understand the thought process in my pea brain that thought she'd be better off if she thought I was dead, and to this day I feel badly, but the end result was that I had no one to go back to. I wasn't worried since there were always plenty of girls available but I hadn't counted on the thousands of guys who'd just spent months in a war returning to the same place, at the same time, as horny as I was, and just as determined to score.

After a 5 hour shower at my apartment, cleaning sand from crevices I had forgotten existed, I took a long nap and woke up ready to hit the bars. My goal was clear – I was going to find someone special beautiful, intelligent, funny and cool. Ok, that's a lie. I wanted someone who would say, "Sure War, let's go! Ravage me you returning hero!"

When I got to the Irish Pub in Sachsenhausen, I realized this was going to be harder than I'd thought. The bar was flooded with returning service members, so the girls there had their choice of guys, and damn, they leveraged it well. At this point I had 3 choices.

1. You join the line for one of the hot chicks – Fuck that. I have zero interest in standing in line with my tongue hanging out just hoping that when I finally get to the front of the line I'm going to hit the right combination and she'll go home with me. It's just ... well, undignified and humiliating. Not just no, but hell no.

2. Give up – Hell with that. There was no way I was going to crawl back to my apartment and

fall asleep after what we'd just been through. Plus, you have to strike while the iron is hot. Many of the girls at the bars were looking for boyfriends and would be off the market after tonight. This was pretty common, by the way. We used to joke that the German girls just wanted to live in the "Land of the Great PX (Post Exchange)".

3. Compromise – Now there's no shame in lowering your expectations in the interest of success. Let the haters hate, but at the end of the evening when I'm having wild rollicking sex with someone new and the alternative is a hooker or "taking care of one's own business", I'll take the fun bouncing girl on top of me every time.

Ok, so I made the decision to cut my losses and score, then scanned the room for someone acceptable. In a dark corner I saw her. Holy sweet mother of god. Smoking ass. Long brown hair. Slender. She was with two girls and I know that can be a pain, but nothing someone of my caliber couldn't surmount. Remember, horny + confident + just came back from a war = success. I grabbed my Beam and Coke and headed over. I don't remember what line I used to broach their defenses, but they laughed, and I turned to see the object of my desire.

Did you know there's a steak in Texas that's 72oz? Yep. Four and a half pounds. The Great Texan Steak House in Amarillo, TX will give it to you for free if you can eat the whole thing, that's how big it is. It puts other steaks to shame. If you finish it, your name is put up on the wall with others who have accomplished the herculean feat. Anyone attempting it eats on a raised table in the center of the restaurant, where everyone there can see someone crazy enough to try to eat a 72oz steak. That's how ridiculously large it is and it's the largest piece of meat I've ever seen.

With the exception of this girl's nose. Holy god. Think of a keel on a sailboat. You know, that thing that extends deep into the water and keeps the boat from tipping over? Pretend some evil genius fused it to this poor girl's face. I felt the wind when she turned to me. It all became clear. Yes, she had a killer body, but there was no way under normal circumstances I could have ignored the nose. Fortunately, these weren't normal circumstances. I kept the shock off my face and continued to charm the three of them, slowly but surely focusing my attention on her.

Her response was gratifying. She was surprised at first, probably because her friends were better looking, albeit chunkier, and I was clearly warming up to her. I did my normal routine of funny and self-deprecating humor and when she snorted in laughter I felt twin blasts of warm air on my cheek. But I didn't care. She was mine and that night she was going help me back into the groove.

Enter my buddy Ron. Good guy, although a tad boring. Girls liked him for about the first couple weeks, then they took off, mostly because while he was tall, dark, and handsome, he was also boring. So things would start off hot and heavy, then things would become strained and slowly taper off to nothing when the girls realized there was really nothing to talk about. I'd seen it happen many times. Anyway, Ron stumbled up, half-lit and irritated that he'd struck out all night. He came up to find out how I was doing and if I'd had any success. He knew my reputation, so when he saw the three girls and me, he arrived at the natural and accurate conclusion. So, he leaned over and in what to him was a stage whisper, bellowed:

"WAR! YOU GONNA BANG THE BITCH WITH THE BEAK?"

I watched her face turn beet red. Her friends looked at Ron in shock. My face fell. In that moment I knew there was no recovery. Her hands flew up to her nose as if to cover it, but that wasn't possible, so she rushed off, her friends in tow.

"No, Ron, I'm not." I said.

By now it was late, too late to try and start over. The hotties were gone, the drunks were sloppy, and dammit, I wasn't getting laid. Thanks Ron, you rat bastard. I vowed to get even.

My chance came less than a month later. Ron had managed to find a really cute girl a few weeks after the incident but she'd already gotten bored of him. I had talked to her a few times and played the clever card, so she already liked me. I can't remember her name so let's call her something good and German. How about Helga? Sure, why not? Anyway, one night a bunch of us were back at the Irish Pub getting our drink on. Ron lumbered around getting Helga drinks while I made her laugh. A few minutes later, he said he had to get up early and was heading out. She told him she was going to stick around for a bit but she'd catch up with him later. Hot Damn! I was in! Not long after Ron left, I asked Helga if she'd mind giving me a ride home. Of course she was glad to help. We got back to my apartment building and I asked if she wanted to come up for a bit.

Now here's the deal. It was nearly 2:00am. Helga was sober as she'd only had a few drinks and those had worn off hours before. She had to work the next day, so she wasn't looking for a place to crash and sleep it off. I didn't have any coffee, hell, I didn't even have a coffee maker back then. She'd been flirting with me all night, light touches, hair flips, coy glances and innuendo. I knew the deal and so did she. We weren't there to hold hands, we were going to have sex and I couldn't wait.

I don't think she made it up the first flight of stairs before attacking me and her clothes were off before we got inside. We were making out like crazy, almost frantically, and I told her my standard line: "I don't have any boundaries. Tell me what you want me to do to you. Anything your sick little mind can think up, I'll do. Just tell me." She paused for a second, looked at me and nodded slowly in thought then a slow smile came over her face. Uh oh…

Her fantasy was forced sex that turns her on so much she can't help but get into it. I had pretend I'd picked her up and wouldn't let her go home, physically restraining her while she tried to get away, then tying her up and having my way with her. Well ok then! It turned out she was strong as hell and I had to actually work at it! It was actually tough keeping her down but at the same time a huge turn-on. Who knew?

I looked around for something to tie her wrists with and all I could find was the belt on my bathrobe. It was standard terrycloth and wouldn't rip, so I tied her up and went to town on her. She was fun as hell, writhing around like crazy, trying to get loose but she went from "Nein, nein nein nein" to "JA JA JA JA" and when she came I'm pretty sure she woke the evil cleaning lady who lived in the room directly beneath mine.

All in all, I was pretty proud of the performance. I untied her and as we were sitting there naked having a drink she noticed her wrists. In all the excitement, my robe had pretty much taken the skin off her wrists. She wasn't bleeding, but she looked like a recently rescued hostage. It was bad. The worst part of the whole thing was there is really only one way to get those marks and everyone who saw them would know exactly how. She took off and I went to bed.

I saw her a few days later at a party and she was there with Ron. Her wrists were bandaged. I managed to get her alone and asked her what the hell had happened. She told Ron she'd fallen down the stairs. He believed her and that was that. I think they lasted another week or so, but it was all downhill from there. I only saw her once again but that's another story.

I repeated this until I left Germany a few months later. I slept with every single one of his girlfriends. And then I'd tell him. He had no real emotional investment in them, so it was just funny. If he had actually liked them I wouldn't have done it, but he was just pissed that he'd wasted all that time priming them and I'd come in and pump them. Several of his "girlfriends" he hadn't actually slept with. So he did all the legwork and I'd get laid.

He got out of the Army and I didn't hear from him for a few years. When I did, I heard he was in the building across the street from the one that was blown up in Oklahoma. He was cut up pretty badly from flying shards of glass and really hasn't been right in the head since. I think he went back into the military, although I'm not entirely sure. I do know he ended up working for Blackwater for a few years and has turned into a badass.

Somehow, I've haven't run into him since, although my friends have. It might be for the best. I'm still kinda irritated at him for cockblocking me that one time. Some things you just can't forgive.

43. THE FEMINIST

Ever met a girl who was nearly perfect but had some psychological issue you just couldn't get over? You really like her, you really want to be with her but you realize you just can't. I seem to attract them – I wish I knew why. Andi was one of these. I met her one night when I was shooting pool at the Pine Crack in Woodstock and she was stunning.

She fit my physical profile, i.e., tall, slender, dark hair, but what drew me to her was that she was wearing a kimono. I mean, how cool is that? Who wears a kimono to a bar who isn't Asian? Anyway, somehow she managed to trick me into shooting doubles with her. I had girls try all the time, not because I'm so stunningly good looking but because I was such a pool shark that if they played with me, they'd have something fun to do the rest of the night. Plus, girls do love a winner. She employed the oldest ruse in the book – "Hey you want a partner?" Why yes, yes I did.

Andi was wired really tightly. Our opponent spent a good 3-4 minutes between shots chalking his cue and it drove her nuts. You could see her getting angrier and angrier each time he dusted the chalk over the tip and cocked his head to re-evaluate the next shot. The worst part was he was horrible and missed almost everything he tried.

I thought it was really funny, not because it didn't bother me, but because she was so obviously losing her mind over it. I patiently waited until he was done missing his shot and ran the table. You could see the tension drain out of her and she looked at me like I was her savior and hero all in one. Go me!

We started talking and I was smitten. She was an utter bitch. Sarcastic, bitter, angry, unhappy, my god, she was perfect! I don't know what it was back then that drew me to horrible women like Andi. Maybe it was the kimono. She'd just gotten out of a long-term relationship and while I listened, I was skeptical the guy was as much a dick as she made him out to be. I didn't matter, of course. I listened politely and kept drinking, shooting and winning.

Over the next weeks we managed to meet at the Crack on a few more occasions and each time we had more and more fun. We became an item and our relationship consisted of drinking, shooting pool, and crazy sex. We didn't really talk that much after the first few weeks, mostly because it turned out she was an incredibly annoying ultra-feminist.

She was in law school and always whining about the glass ceiling, the plight of the woman today, the 75% pay discrepancy, etc. At first I was fine with it, but she just went on and on and on about it. I mean, ok, I know there are some issues, but seriously, aren't there more interesting things to talk about? Spending time with her became tedious, but by the same token, she really got off giving head, and who doesn't like that?

Anyway, I can be a bit of a dick and enjoyed tweaking her. I'd make sexist jokes, make fun of ugly girls, point out the bull dykes and suggest I could turn them, etc. Andi would become furious. It was so easy to set her off and I would do it whenever I got bored. She would get all mad, tell me that my attitude was the reason women had all the troubles they had, then spend the next hour blowing me and telling me how much her Dad was a horrible person.

By the way, when I met him, we got along famously. He was a great guy, a lot like me actually. But I digress. Anyway, our relationship was rocky and I was about done with the whole thing when one day we were chilling in my house and I got hungry. I suggested to her that I needed something to eat and "Dem sammiches ain't gonna make themselves". I thought that was pretty funny. She did not.

She got all wound up and started yelling at me about how I was such a sexist pig, that I knew how important feminism was to her, and that I couldn't possibly love her when I was so comfortable saying such offensive things.

You know that phrase that you don't say, but you really want to, and you know if you say it, things are over? Yeah. I said it.

With all the contempt and frustration months of her whining had built up, I said, "Well, you're pretty much an occasional feminist because I pay for everything."

BACK TO THE STORIES

I hear she's doing well, dating another guy exactly like her father.

44. My Last Fight

I have lost as many fights as I won. I have a nice scar on my upper lip from getting sucker punched. I went down like a sack of potatoes. As I grew up, I realized that I valued my teeth much more than getting in the last word or proving to some anonymous guy in a bar that I was tougher.

It has been many years since I was in a really good knock-down, drag-out fight. I credit my self-preservation and maturity, as well as my wish to stay out of jail. Hey, you never know what can happen, right? Come to think of it, the last fight I was in wasn't really even a fight…

At the time, I was living with my Army buddy, the one who I double-teamed Betty with, and that dumbass loved to fight. Well, he was banned for life from the Pine Crack and I had to go there alone, since it was the closest place with a pool table and the people were cool.

Anyway, it was a slow night and this short little fucker kept annoying me. I was a much better pool player but he kept on talking and just fucking with me.

Now I am a pretty peaceful guy, but this annoying little yapping terrier finally got to me. I told him that we should go outside and discuss this, away from everyone else. My goal was to defuse things and figured that all the eyes might make things worse.

He freaked out and said he wouldn't go outside unless I promised not to hit him. Ok, I promise, you mushroom. Anyway, we went outside and I asked him what the hell he was doing, told him that I was just trying to have some fun and he was being annoying as hell.

He replied that he was just trying to even the playing field, that he knew I was way better than he was and he was just trying to win. I told him I understood, but that wasn't cool and he agreed to stop. We shook hands.

Win, right? Wrong. As soon as we got inside, he says loudly, "AND YOU'RE STILL A FUCKING ASSHOLE!" Well fuck. So I threw him through a bunch of chairs and he left. I told my side of the story and never saw him again.

45. THE PATHOLOGICAL LIAR

In my life, I've only met two people who constantly lied about everything. One of them was my roommate in the Army when I was stationed in Monterey, CA at the Defense Language Institute. My old roommate had finished his training and was moving on and the new guy they assigned me was cool as hell.

"John" was awesome. He could dance his ass off, girls liked him, he was funny, and always had a good story. I was thrilled to have a roommate who wouldn't cramp my style and it's always good to have a wingman. We got along great, never had any problems or arguments, so when he said he'd had a screw-up and the Post Exchange wouldn't cash a check for him, I had no problems cashing it for him. I'd just deposit the check into my account, give him cash, and we'd be square. No problem, right?

It was approaching Christmas and I was trying to figure out how to get back to visit my folks in South Carolina, when he suggested we just drive it.

BACK TO THE STORIES

I figured that would be far cheaper, so John, a third buddy (Carter) and I hopped into the car and headed out. John's car had some problems prior to our leaving, but I cashed a check for him to get it all squared away. We agreed I'd cover the gas and food on the way out, then he'd cover it on the way back. It was just easier that way, right? We left Monterey and drove directly to Kingman, AZ, about 12 or so hours, dropped off Carter, then headed to Wilmington, NC.

We drove in shifts, only stopping for gas and food. I don't know how many tablets of Vivarin and No-Doze I popped, but 36 hours later, we arrived in Wilmington, with a total drive time of slightly over 48 hours. Coast-to-coast in 48 hours is a record I'm sure I'll never beat and by the time we got there, we were wired as hell. John had been telling me how many girls he knew and that he'd hook us up when we got there, so I was stoked.

He was unable to convert. His excuses ranged from "There's really no one here that's cool" (the place was packed) to "She moved." Bored and irritated, we headed back to his house. He went straight to bed, but they opened up a sofa-bed so I figured I'd watch a little TV and then try to get some sleep. I had started to zone out when someone crawled into bed with me. Holy shit, it was his little sister. According to the laws of North Carolina, she was of age, but there were plenty of other states that would have disagreed. Regardless, I was horny, she was hot, and she jumped me. It's really hard to beat the enthusiasm of youth. She'd been flirting with me the whole day so I guess it wasn't completely out of the blue, but nailing your buddy's little sister while you're crashing on his couch could be construed as a bit rude.

Looking back, he deserved it.

The next day, he drove me down to where my parents were and dropped me off. My parents were thrilled to see me so I spent a week or so with them before it was time to head back. John came back down to pick me up, and this was when the trouble started. He had no money. At all. He blamed it on the Army finance team and said he was really sorry, but there was nothing he could do. We still had to get back to California, and there was no way I was going to be a dick and abandon him 2800 miles from home. I didn't have that much money, but soldiers take care of each other. That's the code.

We decided to take the southern route via I-10 for a change of scenery. We hit San Antonio, TX, were pretty burned out but decided we had enough time to make a quick detour to Mexico. I should have known better.

We hit a whorehouse right across the border and had a few drinks, but we had neither the inclination nor the funds to partake of the local delights so we decided to get back on the road. John had been worried about leaving his car, so we ended up driving into Mexico. Bad move.

It was on the way out that the trouble started. John said he was OK to drive, but this claim demanded further review when he plowed into the side of a Mexican's car.

Oh fuck. We had heard stories about soldiers being thrown into Mexican jails so we got out, freaking out. Neither of us spoke Spanish, so we were immediately the center of attention as the Mexican got out of his car and started yelling at us. I was unable to see where we'd hit him. His car was such a beater that I'm pretty sure even he couldn't have pointed to the dent we'd made. As the yelling continued, people started to approach from all directions. I dug into my pocket, took out ALL my cash, handed it to him, said, "No Mas" and told John to get back in and to drive us the fuck out of there. No one chased us, but now we were fully and completely broke. Neither of us had a single dollar.

We crossed the border and slept in the car, then woke up to assess our options. We had enough gas to get to San Antonio, so I told him to point the car there and we'd get to a base where I could cash a check. When we got there, we went on the base and to my utter shock I found I'd been flagged as passing bad checks. What the fuck?!?!?! I knew that was crap and they told me there was nothing they could do.

With no other options, we asked around, and then hit a pawn shop. I had hundreds of cassettes, and I pawned all of them for 25 cents each. "In God We Trust, Inc." by the Dead Kennedys – Gone. AC/DC – Back in Black – Gone. My camera – Gone. Everything was sold. We managed to scare up enough cash to get us back to Kingman, AZ where Carter was waiting to be picked up, based 100% on me selling everything I owned. I would like to point out that John had nothing to sell, so he contributed nothing. He said that he was sorry, but that he'd replace everything I'd had to sell, so I shouldn't worry.

We arrived in Kingman, told Carter about our predicament and I asked if his Mom could cash a check for me, since I couldn't do it myself. She agreed to do it, but made me promise that there was really money in my account, since she couldn't cover it herself. I promised. Newly funded, we headed back to base in Monterey where I was certain we'd work it all out. Well, it turned out John had royally fucked me.

Every single check he had written me was bad. I'd cashed over a thousand dollars' worth of checks for him so when they bounced, the deposits were removed and my account was negative. This meant the check I'd written to my buddy's mom was also bad. That was one of the most humiliating phone calls I'd ever had to make. I didn't have the money to fund my account but I begged, borrowed and hit up all my friends until I could cover the check I'd written to her.

The next day I was told to report to the Platoon Leader. The Army takes bad check writing very seriously, so they were ready to drop the hammer on me for all the checks I'd written. By now I'd figured out that my cool roommate had fucked me so I no longer felt any loyalty to him. I told them everything that had happened, swore out a complaint against him and they told me they would take money out of his paycheck to pay me back. Whew. Well, at least that was something. I decided I should get something to drink and hit the PX for a 6 pack of beer and some wine coolers.

I've always hated beer and since it was against the rules to have hard liquor in the barracks, I wanted something to drink. We were only allowed to have one six pack per person who was 21, but John asked me to pick him up a 6-pack when I was up there. I was still trying to be nice and hadn't learned my lesson.

BACK TO THE STORIES

That night, there was a "Health and Welfare" inspection. When you're in training in the Army, they have surprise inspections to make sure you don't have any contraband, don't have any women in there, and your room isn't completely trashed. Usually I had advance notice from my friends in the office, but this time there was no warning. The Platoon Sergeant came in, opened up the fridge, saw I had a 6-pack of beer and a 6-pack of coolers and turned to John and asked, "How old are you John?"

"20, Sgt."

WHAT THE FUCK? John had even lied about his age.

The next day they brought me back into the office and wrote me up on an Article 15 for having too much alcohol. I lost it. I pointed out that it was my stupid fucking roommate who'd lied, yet again, and it was his. To his credit he admitted it, so they threw out my Article 15, but it was touch and go. See, they'd been trying to catch me for almost 2 years. They all knew I had women in my room. All the time. Stories about my escapades had reached their ears. They were just itching for a chance to finally get me. It was with the greatest reluctance they let me off.

By now, John's name was shit. Everyone had heard that he fucked me over, and I was pretty popular, so people hated him. So he took the only route available to him to win them back. He bought them all pizza. Two to three times a week. With checks. That bounced. Yep, he kept writing bad checks until they finally threw him out of the Army.

So to summarize, he fucked me out of more than a thousand bucks, didn't pay for a trip across the country, nearly got me in serious trouble, lied about his age, got me in even more trouble and then was kicked out of the Army.

But at least I nailed his sister.

46. How I Got My First Book Published

I had just married my wife and we were on our honeymoon driving up the coast of California. I was mostly raised there so I wanted to show her some of the places I'd lived. We went to Disneyland, stayed at the Grand Californian (awesome hotel), and from there, just winged it.

Quick aside: We stayed a few nights in Hollywood, one of my favorite places in the world, but we found a hotel called the Renaissance that was right downtown. That place is my 2nd favorite hotel, so we were doing the whole tourist thing, wandering around, when we noticed a huge crowd. We went to see what was going on and it was the 2nd Star Wars movie. Well, I'm a massive Star Wars fan, so we had to go watch. The stars were pulling up in limos, the fans were going wild, and from down the block, Darth Vader and a bunch of Stormtroopers were coming toward us.

Anyway, I started talking to this guy and turned out he was working there. It was the premiere of Episode 2 but it was for charity, so not the normal type of premiere. The tickets were 500 bucks each, so it would have been 1000 and there were still a couple left that we could have bought. I obviously wanted to go, considering it was freakin' STAR WARS, with the director (in whom I still had faith) and all the stars, but my wife vetoed. She said it was too much money for a movie.

Since we had only been married a week and her mom had died 3 weeks prior, I gave in. Later, I was bumming and explained how much Star Wars had been a part of my youth and how missing it was just crushing. She was really sorry and said that if ever anything else came up that was that important to me, just say Star Wars and she'd give in. Haven't played that card, but it's nice knowing it's there.

So we got back from our honeymoon and about a month later my VP told me that I had resigned. WTF? This is another long story, but basically we got a new VP, she hated me and wanted a crony to have my job. She won, I lost.

I spent the next few years licking my wounded ego and doing project management for various Fortune 50 companies. The reason I'm bringing this up is that right after I "resigned", my wife said she wanted to buy a house.

I told her she was crazy, but her rationale was that if we bought a house and needed to borrow money from our folks, the money wouldn't be thrown away, it would go toward a mortgage, not rent. So we did. That was the beginning of our real estate acquisition.

BACK TO THE STORIES

We lived there a few years, then bought a house in a pretty ritzy area. We bought at a good time and paid 1k over the asking price of 435k. Real estate was booming and our house had increased by 200k in value, so we took out a HELOC and bought a computer store. Everything was going swimmingly until the market crashed. We were in desperate straits, losing 10k a month, but managed to turn everything around in the space of about 6 months.

This is where the book comes in and thanks for your patience. My wife took notes on everything we did to fix our broken business. I said, "Hey, you should write a book about this. I think other people could benefit from the shit we just went through." Well, she's nuts, so she threw together a few chapters and showed it to me.

It was awful. Oh sure, the information was there but no one would ever read it. Fortunately, she'd was married to me :) I took her chapters and re-wrote them to be fun to read. Then I bought a book on how to get published. It's called "The Writers Market" and tells you exactly what to do. So we did that.

We wrote up an introduction, targeted the publishing houses, did our market research and sent off our chapters. Nothing. Absolutely nothing. So we said, Fuck it, it was worth a try. Flash forward 7 months. I got a call on my cell from a (V)ery (P)olite (W)oman:

VPW: "Hi, my name is Eileen from XXX Publishing House. I'm the managing editor and we want to publish your book."

Me: "HAHAHA. Aw, that's so cute. How much is it going to cost us for you to 'publish' us?"

THE WARLIZARD CHRONICLES

VPW: "Oh no sir, this isn't a vanity publishing house. We're a real publisher. If you're interested, I'll overnight the contracts."

Well, fuck me. Yep, it was real. She sent over the contracts, we had our lawyer look them over and we signed. The book came out in March and we've been doing interviews (mostly radio) ever since.

47. MUTTFACE

War sucks. You're away from the comforts of home, you're in a foreign land, and the locals are shooting at you. Because of this, you have to rely strongly on the people in your unit. If you don't have that support, it's the worst thing possible, because aside from the lack of friendship, the loneliness and the boredom, you don't ever want someone to pause when you need rescuing. You want your squad members to jump into a hail of bullets to rescue you if necessary, and not think about that time you stole his girlfriend, ate his last donut, or got the promotion he deserved.

We were a bunch of bickering children when we arrived in Saudi Arabia. Our unit was comprised of German and Russian Linguists, Direction Finding equipment, radio communication jammers, and some support staff. We had no idea why we were there and were pretty irritated about the whole thing. This led to constant fighting over stupid shit and general unfocused anger. It got to the point where we would jump someone's shit over the slightest provocation. Didn't matter what it was, but we didn't have an outlet for our frustration, so any target would do. Enter Sgt. "Crum", aka "Muttface". I forget who made up the name (I did), but it was descriptive and caught on. Sgt. Crum was assigned to our Battalion after we arrived in Saudi Arabia, didn't know anyone, but was assigned a squad and told to get to work. She told one of the more experienced soldiers in her squad, "Sally" to do something stupid, Sally impatiently told her to go fuck herself, and Muttface reported her for insubordination.

You have to understand, we took care of EVERYTHING internally. The idea of reporting someone for being rude was just crazy. You would take the person somewhere private and you'd work it out. I'm not saying that you'd necessarily get in a fight, but you'd let them know in no uncertain terms where they stood. While it's true you respect the rank, not the person, in a combat situation, you need both. People who don't earn respect tend to have a very difficult and short existence.

Anyway, Muttface went to the Company Commander and filed a formal report. He was forced to deal with it officially and Sally received a Field Grade Article 15, just one step below a court martial. I guess the civilian equivalent would be a serious misdemeanor vs. a felony. Normally, this would have been dealt with less formally, but we were about to deploy into Iraq and the Commander needed to ensure that all orders were followed, immediately, without question. He had to make an example and Sally was demoted from Sergeant, E-5, to Specialist, E-4. Shock waves radiated throughout the Battalion. The bitching and whining stopped, because no one wanted to lose hard-earned rank and pay.

From that point on, Muttface was fucked. Sally was hot, popular, good at her job, and incidentally, the best shot in the battalion with an M-60. If Muttface had taken Sally aside, ripped her head off and given her extra duty, no one would have cared. It would have been seen as cracking the whip and keeping your troops in line. By going to the Company Commander, it showed weakness, poor judgment, and a total lack of social savvy. After that, no one would talk to her unless asked a direct work question. No one would eat with her. No one would look at her. She was completely shunned, even by the troops who reported to her. They enacted a so-called "White Mutiny" where they would do precisely what she said, but nothing more. They showed no initiative and required her to give them precise instructions which they would follow, regardless of the outcome. Things got worse and worse, but what could she do? Go back to the Company Commander and complain that her soldiers were mean to her? He was already pissed at her so she risked losing her job and having her evaluation reflect that during a war situation, she couldn't lead.

One day, my partner-in-crime, Sgt. Dirk and I were walking by her tent and heard crying from inside. Awwww, Sgt. Muttface was sad? How about grow a pair and act like a soldier. You were Miss Authority when you fucked over Sally, now you're all alone and wish someone would like you. Dirk said, "I feel kinda badly for her. She's fucked and nothing can change. No one will ever like her and her entire tour of duty here is going to suck." He always was a sucker for a damsel in distress.

That got me thinking... Could I change it around? Could I make her popular? I'd need Dirk's help, but I thought it might be possible. Over the next day or so, I came up with the plan and when it seemed bulletproof, I told it to Dirk. He was down for making the attempt, especially since we were so bored. It broke down into a 3-pronged approach:

1. Build up Muttface – We needed people to think she was actually ok.
2. Break down Sally – People had to believe that Sally deserved everything she got.
3. Reverse the White Mutiny – Muttface's team had to start to work really hard for her.

Of course, first we had to get Muttface on our side, but that was easy. She was so hated and was just looking to anyone for approval that when two of the coolest guys in the Battalion just started talking to her and being nice, she didn't even question it. She ate it up.

We told her that the whole thing was unfair, that she'd be in the right the whole time and that anyone with a shred of objectivity could see she wasn't getting a fair shake. We furthermore clarified that our mission would be to make sure that people saw her side. You should have seen her light up. I thought she was going to lose it right then and there, so Dirk and I took off. As soon as we left the tent, the muffled sobbing started, but this time it was from happiness.

BACK TO THE STORIES

First, we started bringing up Muttface to the other people in the Battalion, saying we'd gotten to know her a bit and she wasn't actually that horrible. We agreed that what she'd done to Sally was a cunt move, but outside of that, she wasn't that bad a person. We were met with great skepticism, but we had quite a bit of credibility so people started to look at her differently.

A few days later I pointed out that it must be really horrible to come into a new unit and have one of your new troops tell you to go fuck yourself, but no doubt, Muttface's reaction was over the top. Our response might have been a bit harsh. People grudgingly agreed, but they weren't sure.

Casually, when I was having lunch with a squad leader in her Platoon, I said I'd heard that the Standard Operating Procedure in Muttface's old unit was to immediately alert the Commander to any breach of discipline, because he was such a stickler for rules. So while she probably shouldn't have done it in a brand new unit, we could see how it could have happened. People stopped looking at her like she was Saddam Hussein and began to start talking to her.

Next, we started pointing out to people that what Sally had done, immediately jumping in the face of a new Sgt. wasn't the smartest thing to do, but it was understandable, based on how stupid the order had been. We never tried to change anyone's mind, we just planted seeds and let them grow. A little later, we noted that Sally was awesome, but sometimes she could be a bit headstrong, after all really hot chicks often have a sense of entitlement. Ugly girls are usually jealous of attractive girls, so we had a receptive audience. I played on their insecurities and wondered aloud if Crum were reacting to an ugly girl giving her an order or if the order were really that stupid. And calling her "Muttface" was pretty cruel, anyway. Did anyone remember how it got started? Was Sally the one who'd started it?

One of the uglier girls thought that she might have heard Sally say it first. Well, that put a whole new spin on the situation. It wasn't long before another girl suggested that Sally had always been a bit of a bitch and people had become used to her getting her way or facing her wrath. But her demotion wasn't deserved was it? I asked the group of girls why Sally had been promoted and they hadn't. The tide turned and they all agreed that they were tired of pretty girls getting promoted when more competent soldiers who were better at their jobs languished. Maybe that's what this had all been about. It was really just another example of a spoiled bitch throwing a hissy fit and getting her just desserts, wasn't it? Come to think of it, FUCK SALLY, that entitled bitch!

It was amazing, watching the shift in public opinion. Two weeks before, Muttface had been hated, now people were referring to her by her real name, "Crum", even in private. In public, they started being nice to her and Sally just couldn't understand how she'd gone from Hero to Bitch in less than two weeks. The final piece of the puzzle was to fix Crum's relationship in the Battalion. I'm most proud of this part, by the way.

I approached her squad and asked if I could speak to them privately. I held a secret meeting one night while everyone else was asleep and said I understood that

Crum was a horrible leader, but that they were fucking up their own careers by trying to destroy hers. I said that the Battalion wouldn't know that she sucked, they would only know that she had a squad of complete fuckups and the best thing to do would be to ship them off somewhere they couldn't do any damage. I postulated that loading ammo didn't require much intelligence and I knew there were many jobs within the Battalion like that. Dirty jobs. Building bathrooms, burning shit, KP, all of those were tasks that had to be done and someone had to do them. Why not use the fuckups? Plus, did they really want to go into combat unprepared? They were really doing themselves a disservice by not doing everything they could to get ready.

I saw they were starting to agree with me, so hit them with the knockout. The best way to get rid of Crum was to make the Battalion think that she was awesome, so they'd move her to a job in the HQ. This hit home, because we'd seen it happen many times before. Bust your ass, get noticed, you'd be working for the Colonel and your life would be sweet. It wasn't fair, but dammit, if they could get rid of her, they'd all be together and they wouldn't have to put up with her bullshit. Plus, they were tired of looking like a bunch of fuckwits who couldn't do the simplest task without supervision. We all agreed that they were going to do everything by the book, quickly and accurately, but more importantly, they would make sure they'd tell anyone who would listen what a great squad leader she was.

THE WARLIZARD CHRONICLES

I would like to point out, all of this was utter and complete bullshit. Crum was an annoying bitch. Sally rocked. There was no way Crum would be transferred out during a goddam war and thinking so was just moronic. But it worked. In just a few short weeks, everyone loved Crum, agreed that Sally had gotten what she deserved, and we heard through the grapevine that the Battalion was really impressed by the way Crum had turned around her squad. Dirk and I sat back one night on guard duty and reflected that by the application of a bit of logic and psychology we had completely changed someone's life. It wasn't fair, but then again, neither is life.

Dirk had spent the last few weeks with Crum almost non-stop. He was always there to agree with her ideas (which he'd fed her earlier) when she talked with her squad, laugh at her jokes, and support her utterly. I guess it was inevitable that they'd start fucking. If you remember Dirk from my other stories, you'll know that he fucked anything that moved, regardless of how pretty she was. He wanted approval and Muttface gave it to him. She looked at him like he was her savior, the one who turned a horrible life into a great one and he was her hero. I got zero credit for being the mastermind behind the whole thing, naturally, because she couldn't know it all went down. They started spending more and more time in her tent, trying to be discreet, but Dirk gave me the gory details. At first.

The fucker fell for her. I realized it first when he started acting really strangely around me when I called her Muttface. I was sure when he asked me to call her by her first name. I flipped. "Goddam it. Seriously?

You bought our bullshit? We made it all up! She's an idiot!" He wouldn't listen and told me that I just didn't know her, that she was really great, a kind soul and more crap like this. I pointed out that he was married and his wife was actually pregnant back in Germany. He said it wasn't like that, he'd never leave his wife, but we were 7000 miles away and he really cared for Crum.

What was I to do? I let it go and a few months later his wife was in an accident in Germany and they shipped him back. When Crum got back to Germany, she told him she'd go with him and all he had to do was ask. He told her there was no way he could abandon his wife and unborn kid, but that he'd love her always. Crum left, and with the stellar evaluation from her time in the Gulf got a nice promotion.

Whatever.

Now there's one thing you might be wondering... Aside from the fun of the experiment, why in the hell was I willing to shred Sally? What kind of dick move was that? I almost hesitate to tell you, but I'd always had a crush on her and she'd always blown me off. When everyone turned on her, there was always one person who was there for her, taking her side in private and telling her how fucked up it was that everyone was Crum's friend. She needed someone on whom she could rely. After years of people sucking up to her, the black void of hatred was too much for her to take and I was the only person keeping it at bay. It was inevitable that the relationship would become physical.

So yes, I destroyed one person, elevated another, lied my ass off, architected a mutiny, destroyed it, and got an absolute idiot promoted, all to get laid.

48. MY FIRST JOB

Ok, so my Dad decided that it was high time I learned the value of money, so unbeknownst to me, he called a local farmer and told him that he would pay the farmer to give me a job. I was 9. Dad told me that I should go down to this guy and ask him for a job. I hated this guy, but my parents were really strict and I wasn't exactly in the position to argue. Here's why I hated this guy.

Flash back about 6 months. We lived in a little town called Morgan Hill in California and we had a tiny house on 4 acres of land. I had 2 dogs, Sugar and Spice, German Shepherds and I loved them to pieces. Unfortunately, they weren't house dogs -- they pretty just ran around and do whatever they wanted. Regardless, they'd hang with me when I went hiking and I thought they were cool as hell. Well, Spice would run around pretty frequently since he wasn't chained up or anything and he liked to mess with the neighbor's rabbits. He had killed a few of ours by pulling their hair through their cage and it was pretty gruesome, but hey, he was a dog, right? Anyway, he started sniffing around Barney Foster's house (the farmer from above) and Mr. Foster came to my dad and complained. My dad told him that we'd try to keep the dogs away from his farm, but he should do what he had to.

I was unaware of this conversation.

So Spice took off one day and came home shot up. Turned out Mr. Foster decided the easiest way to deal with the problem was to shoot my dog with a shotgun.

He was badly wounded and the question of taking him to the vet never came up. My dad took me and Spice out back, we dug a hole, and we put him down. I felt so badly. My dog was in a hole, looking up at me like I could make things better and then my dad shot him in the head. I know we were broke and there weren't any other options, but that fucking Mr. Foster didn't have to shoot my dog.

Anyway, I walked down to Mr. Foster's house, per my dad's instructions, and told him I was looking for a job. He said he had work and asked me how much I thought I should be paid. Well, I'd never been asked this before and really had no idea what money was worth. So I thought to what I would buy with the money and the first thing that came to mind was the little red paper roll of caps. Most of you probably never heard of these, but basically it was like a very tiny roll of toilet paper but each sheet has a small amount of gunpowder in a dot in the middle. You thread them into a cap gun and when the hammer drops on the gunpowder, it makes a little bang.

A box of caps was 15 cents, and I wanted them, so I told Mr. Foster I thought I was worth 15 cents an hour.

Not the last time I undervalued my worth. So he put me to work cleaning out his pig-pens. His pigs slept in a doghouse, so I had to crawl in there with a broom and clean it out. I did this all day, as well as other labor-intensive chores and at the end of the day, walked home with about a dollar.

I've told that story for years, but there was one piece of the puzzle I only learned recently. My dad paid my salary. He told Mr. Foster that he would cover my pay to the tune of 50 FUCKING CENTS AN HOUR. So Mr. Foster, the guy who killed my dog, made 35 cents an hour off me while I worked for him.

But hey, I learned the value of 15 cents.

49. NEVER SETTLE.

WARLIZARD:

How many times have you met a couple and thought to yourself, "I can't see why they're together. They don't really seem to like each other, they have nothing in common, they spend all their time apart, so what's the point?"

My wife's theory is that when people graduate high school or college, they marry the person they're currently dating. It's like musical chairs – the music stops, get married. It always makes me sad to think that someone could commit to someone without actively wanting to build a life with them, not just someone *like* them.

When I was 16 years old, I made a list of exactly what I wanted in a wife. I enumerated everything that was important to me, from the way she would look, to her education, her sense of humor, how many languages she'd speak, and even what countries she would have visited. It sounds cold and calculating, but I always knew what I wanted and I wasn't willing to settle until the girl was just perfect. Betty wasn't, although I didn't know just how bad things would go, and one of the primary reasons I broke up with her, aside from the fact that she was a freak, was I knew that I couldn't promise I'd be with her forever. I had almost given up hope of ever finding the perfect girl until the day my wife-to-be walked into my office on a job interview.

I was working in NY as a software development manager and the Systems Analysis manager was hiring a contractor to work for him. Since this new person's work would directly affect my team, they would have to interview with me and I had approval over whether or not they would be hired.

The SA manager approached me and said he had a great girl that was smart as hell and frighteningly competent, but she would only be working a few weeks before she took a month long vacation. I vetoed right then and there. No one is good enough to be useful immediately and we had a deadline to hit. Having someone come on, start to learn, then leave for a month was simply unacceptable.

He said this girl was different, that she could do the job and would be more useful than trying to get someone less skilled, that if I'd just give her a chance, he thought I'd like her. I still vetoed. He gave me her credentials, said she had a degree in Electrical Engineering from Cornell and had worked at one of the top 6 consulting firms in the world. I still didn't care, but he bugged me until I grudgingly agreed to interview her. I had no intention of giving my blessing, but it was worth 30 minutes of my time to get him to shut the hell up.

TORDAK (THE WIFE):

Most Information Technology recruiters are morons. Usually, they don't give you enough information to be prepared for an interview and you walk in blind. Less frequently, and just as bad, they give you way too much. This was one of those rare times.

The recruiter called me and said I almost had the job. I was exceedingly qualified for the position, the hiring manager loved me, the team wanted me and there was just one more hurdle. There was this prick that was trying to veto my job because I needed some time off. She went on at length about how much he didn't want me on the team, how involved he would be with the project and what a dick he could be. Then she said I had an interview with him the next day at 9am. Seriously? Is that really the way to send someone into an interview?

I told her that this much information could only cause one of two things to happen. One – if she were talking to a normal person, she would have just stressed that person out so much that the interview would go badly. Knowing someone hates you before they even see you doesn't give you warm fuzzies. Most people would be so nervous it wouldn't matter how qualified they were.

The other option was that the person is so confident in her own abilities and so insensitive to other people that she just wouldn't care, so telling her wouldn't accomplish anything. Fortunately, I am the latter. I resolved that I would destroy this interview and the prick who stood in my way.

WARLIZARD:

Holy fuck. I sat in my office and tried not to stare at the girl who had just walked in. She was tall, slender, wore a tight blue suit with brass buttons and had a 1000 watt smile. Dark long hair, perfectly made up, as together as anyone I'd ever met in my life, this girl was absolutely stunning.

Fuck me. I could barely think, let alone interview her. No one told me she was hot. All they said was that she would be good at her job.

Think, War, think. I stumbled through the interview, asking my normal random questions to see if she'd be able to do the job and ended up by asking her how the hell she thought she could come on for a few weeks, leave, come back, and still be more effective than someone who'd been there the whole time.

She said, "I'm that good."

Fuck me. I thanked her for her time, stood up indicating the interview was over, shook her hand, and told her we'd let her know.

TORDAK:

I **am** that good – not at everything, but at pattern recognition, which is all systems analysis really is - I haven't met better.

I could see why the recruiter warned me though. It was obvious from War's ADHD interview style he was used to throwing candidates (and probably recruiters) off. Jumping from topic to topic, mixing in technical questions, with random comments and opinions probably gave him the upper hand in most business meetings... After all, most people can't easily jump from topic to topic without feeling flustered. But in the first five minutes I had it figured out.

All I had to do was relax, answer succinctly and maybe a bit more cocky than I would normally answer and I would have the job. By the end of the interview I knew it had gone well and that I could work with him. It turned out that was an understatement. Within a few weeks, we were finishing each other's sentences, which is awkward when you "just work together".

WARLIZARD:

The day I met Tordak I broke up with my girlfriend. There just wasn't any point in continuing the relationship. Oh, my current girlfriend was hot, fun, and dynamite in bed, but once I'd met Tordak, I knew I was going to marry her. I told my friends I was done dating, that I'd found "The One", and that I was going to do everything I could to convince her I was the guy for her.

This is complex when you work with someone. I knew the rule about dipping your pen in the company ink, but somehow I figured it just wouldn't matter.

The next year was hell. She was in a relationship and I figured that anyone who could score someone this awesome had to be a truly stellar guy. I played it cool and we became friends, but more than one person told me how perfect we were for each other.

I took this opportunity to grill her about everything she wanted, what she believed, what her goals were, and where she thought her life was going. Since I was just some guy she worked with, she was completely forthcoming. After all, she had nothing to prove to me so she just told me the truth.

My intentions were not honorable.

TORDAK:

"So, how many kids do you want?" I remember where we were when he asked me that. Our company had a small cafeteria and we were sitting downstairs talking over some very bad coffee. Why do I remember? This is an odd question from most people – guys don't usually have the nerve to bring this up even after a few months of dates - but it is even odder from someone you work with. My normal instinct was to go into "date mode" and answer that I wanted "two" (we all know that is the safe answer – I think the rule is one boy and one girl). But, fuck it, I just work with this guy, it's none of his business and it doesn't matter anyway. So, I looked at him and answered the politically incorrect, "Four – all girls if I can swing it".

In many ways it was like the interview never ended. There were lots of random, unrelated questions that were just thrown out from time to time. At first I think I was a bit vague, but as the questions persisted, I became more and more candid. Why not? In a few months, I think he asked almost everything, but "gawd-faw-bid" he was throwing one of his many "work" parties. Inviting me was one question he never seemed to remember to ask.

WARLIZARD:

I still had some pride left, and there was no way I was going to let her know how crazy I was about her.

What, am I some pathetic loser longing from afar while she built a life with some moron who didn't deserve her?

Hell no, she didn't get to come to my parties. I like to get wrecked and didn't feel like professing my eternal love to a work colleague only to have her freak out. It's hard enough working with someone who's crazy about you, it's even harder working with someone when you've made a fool out of yourself in front of them.

I continued my PSYOPS campaign, learning everything I could about her, being her friend, enjoying her company at work, busting my ass, and one day the director called me into his office and told me the company was moving our division to Arizona.

Fuck.

My time was limited. I knew I'd be moving in a few months and she'd be out of my life forever. I was madly in love with her and realized that if I didn't act soon, my window of opportunity would close and I'd be back to banging skanks and regretting I'd never sacked up and told her how I felt.

The problem was she knew I was a dog. She had heard my stories, knew I had a history of instability where women were concerned, so just telling her that we should date wasn't an option. Why would she choose me, especially since I was leaving for Arizona and her whole family was in NY? Realistically, there was only one play. Go big or go home.

I took her out to lunch at a little pizza joint and dropped the bomb. I said I was crazy in love with her, that we were perfect for each other, that I wanted to spend the rest of my life with her and that I thought we should get married.

TORDAK:

I never did get to try that pizza. We went back about ten years later and the restaurant was gone. Oh well. It couldn't have been that good.

The company was moving and contractors are always the first to go. I had turned down a full time senior position in Arizona, so I knew I would be laid off soon. War had become a good friend, but he had never asked me to go to lunch with him alone, so I figured he was giving me "the news". What I was not prepared for was a proposal. I stopped eating and frankly froze (if he was trying to finally win that "non sequitur" contest he did… I was speechless). I didn't know what to say even though I was quite familiar with the options – yes or no.

But there was no way he could have really expected me to say "yes" – right? Sure, I admired his wit, his way of thinking, his confidence, but without a date, without a kiss? It wasn't reasonable. I needed to know more about him and even if I wanted to, I was still in another relationship so it wasn't like I was really free to answer anyway. So, I told him that I would need some time.

He told me that there was an 80-90% chance we would be married and live happily ever after.

Looking back, the oddest part about that lunch was that it never occurred to me to say no.

WARLIZARD:

The rest, as they say, is history. We started dating in earnest, but not the kind of dating where you see a movie or grab dinner. She wanted to know if I were the man she would marry and I answered every question she asked with no evasion. We were together constantly right up until the time I left for Arizona.

Still, she wasn't convinced. She said, "Fuck that, I'm not moving to AZ, my whole family is in NY. I'll marry you but you need to come back."

So she took an interview in the city 9/11/2001 and was there when the planes took out the Towers. She stood there, freaking out, smoke everywhere, wondering how the hell she'd get home. Fortunately, her Dad had retired from the police in NYC and was working for the customs department, so he had a Federal ID as well as the juice to get past the NYPD. He drove in to the city, picked her up, and brought her home.

Quick Aside: She called me from downtown and was flipping the fuck out. I had just seen the towers collapse and was losing my shit as well. Anyway, once I knew she was ok, I stopped worrying. The next night, she was going on and on and on about how horrible it was, how scary it was, how everyone was losing their minds, how far she had to walk in her interview shoes to get to her dad's old police station etc.

Well, I screwed up a bit. I kind of blew her off. I thought she was over-reacting because she had been drinking and was just blathering on and on. I mean, I saw lots of crazy stuff, so how bad could it have been? Well, anyway, turned out she lost a bunch of friends in the towers and she wasn't drunk. I took shit from that miscalculation for years...

Anyway, she was freaked out as hell and her mom told her to get her ass out to AZ. She moved out, took a

6-month lease in the same apartment complex I was living in and figured one of two things would happen: We would be married in 6 months or she'd be flying back to NY.

May 4th, 2002, we were married. We have been married almost 9 years, have 3 kids, and are currently driving around the country and having the time of our lives.

Looking back, there were many times I could have given up. I could have left her in NY. I could have pussied out and remained silent. Hell, all of my friends told me I was crazy. Everyone knows you can't just propose. It's absurd. But I didn't listen because I knew what I wanted and wouldn't accept anything less. I went for it and because of that, I've never been happier.

So when someone tells me they've been dating someone for 5 years and are thinking about moving in together, I tell them it's time to break up. You already know if it's real. If it takes you 5 years to begin to consider a real relationship, you may as well go find someone else. Never settle on someone just because they are convenient. Wait until the right one comes along.

And hey, if you don't find her, you can always get yourself a nice Russian Trophy bride.

AFTERWARD

If you've made it this far, I salute you. You probably think I'm an utter child who just does whatever he wants, and you might be right. I'm a dumbass. I like chocolate milk, playing in the desert, video games, and blowing shit up.

I still think not wearing a bra is sexy. I like road trips, "South of the Border", Disneyland, and waffles shaped like Mickey Mouse. I never grew up, but in the end I have a family that loves me and that I love. My wife lets me be who I am and doesn't try to make me into someone I'm not. With that said...

When I told my wife that I was considering writing down some of my better stories and she first said, "FUCK NO! I don't want the kids reading them!" I have been specifically forbidden from telling my sons about most of my Army exploits and it's her opinion I should be dead many, many times over.

But I wouldn't have any of them if I'd spent my life scared of the big world out there. So take a piece of advice from someone who's been around the block a bit:

ONE LAST STORY

Go out. Explore. Live. See new worlds and stretch yourself.

Just don't tell your kids.

Made in the USA
Lexington, KY
31 January 2012